HAVE YOU [...]
DISAPPOINTED [...]

- Do you always seem to give more in a relationship than you get?
- Do you like the chase but get bored because the passion never lasts?
- Are you attracted to unavailable, mean, or indifferent men?
- Do you feel as if men don't want to commit to you?

TRY A NEW PLAN OF ACTION!

REBECCA SYDNOR's
proven way of

MAKING LOVE HAPPEN

"Among San Francisco women who boast six-figure incomes, sessions with Sydnor are becoming what Jane Fonda workouts were five years ago."

Harper's Bazaar

Now you can learn the proven techniques and strategies which, up until now, have only been available to the privileged attendees of Rebecca Sydnor's popular Romance Management Workshops. Rebecca Sydnor's plan of action leaves nothing to chance and, just as it has worked for countless others, it can work for you.

GET READY TO DISCOVER
THE ULTIMATE JOY
OF LOVING AND BEING LOVED!

"Rebecca Sydnor is the San Francisco marriage guru!"

Nanette Asimov, *San Francisco Chronicle*

"She is the high priestess of matrimony."

Wayne Freedman, Channel 4 News, San Francisco

MAKING LOVE HAPPEN

REBECCA SYDNOR

AVON BOOKS ◆ NEW YORK

AVON BOOKS
A division of
The Hearst Corporation
1350 Avenue of the Americas
New York, New York 10019

Copyright © 1989 by Rebecca Sydnor
Published by arrangement with British American Publishing, Ltd.
Library of Congress Catalog Card Number: 89-35730
ISBN: 0-380-71401-9

The British American Publishing edition contains the following Library of Congress Cataloging in Publication Data:

Sydnor, Rebecca, 1955–
    Making love happen : the smart love approach to marriage in the '90s / Rebecca Sydnor.
        p.   cm.
1. Courtship—United States.   2. Mate selection—United States.
3. Single women—United States—Attitudes.   I. Title.
HQ801.S97   1989
646.7'7—dc20   89-35730

First Avon Books Printing: September 1991

AVON TRADEMARK REG. U.S. PAT. OFF. AND IN OTHER COUNTRIES, MARCA REGISTRADA, HECHO EN U.S.A.

Printed in the U.S.A.

RA   10 9 8 7 6 5 4 3 2 1

Contents

To Neal,
I'll be loving you always

Acknowledgments

This book is dedicated to my husband Neal. From my first workshop to my book contract, he's been my biggest fan. Without his support, encouragement and Love, *Making Love Happen* would never have happened.

A special thanks to Cynthia Traina for creating the opportunity for this book to be written. Her enthusiasm, encouragement and great marketing skills were fundamental in the successful establishment of my career. Charlotte Knabel, my first editor, did an excellent job organizing and polishing the text, and our daily phone conversations kept me on track and always gave me something to laugh about. She was a pleasure to work with.

My second editor, Margaret Mirabelli, got me through some tough deadlines and was patient and understanding about working with a first time author. Kevin Clemente of British American Publishing was charismatic, thoughtful, and always available to answer questions and offer encouragement. Even more importantly, he believed in me and made it possible for me to write this book. Kathleen Murphy did a great job of attending to all the last minute details necessary to get this book to the printers.

I owe special thanks to my family. My sister, Margie Mchann, gave me hope when I was discouraged and was always willing to look over the manuscript and offer fresh insights. My brother David's funny postcards and answering machine conversations kept me in contact with the rest of the world while in hibernation. My Dad, Dr. E. W. Sydnor always offered his support.

I would also like to thank the following people who have contributed greatly to my career and the creation of this book: Wayne Freedman, of the Channel 4 news in San Francisco, who did fabulous news pieces on my workshop that went national and led to my book contract; Alex Bennet, who taught me it's okay to be controversial; Arthur Bruzzone, who pushed me a bit when I needed it; and James Scalise, whose business savvy has been invaluable to me.

Other people who offered their support during different stages of the manuscript include: Sylvia Schlosser, therapist and close friend, who convinced me I could do whatever I set my mind to. Her contributions, particularly in regards to the introduction of the book, were invaluable; Pat Haddock for her excellent work on the proposal and early drafts. Other people who offered their encouragement include: Cora and Bob Storey, Ricky Rafner, Shelly and Myra Freisinger, Anna Bromley, Dottie and Krista Yee, Dan Miller, Gracie and Phil Dickler, Michael and Jamie Dickler, Lucy Anne, Preston and Paige Easely, my assistant Barbara Johnson, Jordan Hart, and Cynthia Michalis.

Introduction

SEVEN YEARS AGO I was burned out on the singles scene. I'd had my share of dead-end relationships and disappointments with men, but was trying not to give up totally. My life wasn't empty without a man. I owned a business and had plenty of friends, but I knew I was missing something by not having someone special to share my life with. This vague feeling of discontent hung over me as it did many of my friends who concentrated on their careers or outside interests rather than dwelling on their lack of a meaningful relationship.

I was accepting the fact that I might end up living my life alone when I decided to return to school to complete my undergraduate degree in psychology and consider becoming a therapist. In the process, during my senior year of college, I stumbled into a course on the psychology of love that changed my outlook on love and relationships forever. I realized it was possible to have more control over the destiny of a relationship, to learn behaviors conducive to moving a courtship forward beyond the initial dating stages to commitment, and even marriage.

After discovering the psychology of love, I knew that I had found the niche I had been searching for. So many of the women in my life, including myself, had been floundering because of a lack of formal education in how to manage their romances. I realized that if other women knew about the psychology of romance, and how it could benefit them in a practical sense, they'd be as eager to learn about it as I was. I researched everything I could on the subject and designed specific strategies to put into effect in my own love life. In the process, I combined the psychological approach of my educational background with my business management skills and demystified the process of how to find a mate. Soon I was getting dramatic results. Within a year I was married to Neal, a man who is everything I was seeking in a mate. Friends began to notice and asked me to offer coaching and workshops. I decided to call my work "Romance Management" because I was teaching women how to manage the outcome of their romances just as they might manage their careers or education. I even trademarked the term Romance Management to use as the name of my company, which specializes in romance and courtship development through private coaching and workshops.

Because Romance Management strives to bring to light self-defeating past patterns, and unresolved issues which may need to be worked through, many women see me in conjunction with a therapist in order to fully benefit from the Romance Management process.

After I decided to take a chance, follow my intuition, and focus my energy entirely on the concept of Romance Management, I soon began receiving a great deal of national media exposure, which attracted the attention of many people who felt Romance Management should be shared with women all over the country so that they could benefit as well. As a result of all the interest and opportunities that came my way, I took a sabbatical from a graduate program in psychology to write this book and offer the Romance Management approach to any woman who is ready to take control of her love life.

For me, feminism means the empowerment of women. I feel that my work with women and this book reflect that philosophy, though I realize not everyone will agree with my definition, approach, or outlook. Regardless of what your personal philosophy may be, I hope you will read this book with an open mind and incorporate whatever works for you into your present lifestyle. Remember, if what you've been doing in the past hasn't gotten you the desired romantic results, it may be time to try a different approach. Romance Management allows you to do just that. After all, what could be more liberating than taking control of your love life rather than just waiting for it to happen?

Wishing you a fine romance,
REBECCA SYDNOR

MAKING LOVE HAPPEN

STOP DREAMING AND TAKE CHARGE OF YOUR LOVE LIFE

The trouble with some women is they get all excited over nothing and then they marry him.

—CHER

I ALWAYS dreamed the right man would come along. When he never showed up, I realized my prince must have been side-tracked. Playing Sleeping Beauty wasn't going to make things happen, so it was time to take matters into my own hands. I decided to go out and find the right man. I knew he was out there somewhere, it was just a matter of looking in the right place, but I had no idea where to begin.

First, I examined my options. I could move to another part of the country, such as Alaska, where the ratio of men to women was more encouraging than San Francisco. I knew of other women who had moved and were now married, but I didn't want to move just for that reason. I could take a second look at former boyfriends. But I rejected this idea straight away. I had dismissed those men for the right reasons the first time and did not have to repeat my mistakes. I took my last option, to form a campaign to find the right man, here where I lived and wanted to stay, in San Francisco. I began with no clear idea how to conduct this search, but I set about the task with the same determination and organization that I had earlier applied to my business career. Although I thought I could trust intuitive powers, I had to face the fact that they hadn't worked in the past. I wanted a method that was not only logical and efficient but guaranteed to work.

I felt that bars weren't good places to find potential mates. While health clubs and organizations were more promising, they required too much of my time. I wanted to find a large pool of likely candidates within a short period of time. So I followed a proven American method that has successfully united seekers with the sought-after for years: I advertised. And lo and behold, my mate came to me faster than certain outfits I've ordered from Spiegel!

This is the ad that I placed:

Blonde Belle Seeks Beau
Attractive blonde belle, 26, 5'7", 125 lbs. complete with soft drawl, pale skin, and parasol, seeks the Rhett of her

**dreams. If you're an attractive, athletic W/M 30–40, 5'11"
or taller, financially secure, emotionally stable, and curious
enough to answer this ad, I'd like to show you a little
Southern hospitality.**

More than 70 men responded! I was astounded. Even more
astonishing, ten of the 70 were likely candidates. I set about
meeting and interviewing each of those ten men, and so narrowed
the field to the three most likely choices. One year later I married
one of them, and it would be hard to find someone better.

When my women friends found out I had placed an ad,
they were flabbergasted. None of them would ever have done
that, they declared. All were more concerned about feeling embarrassed than about remaining single. Not surprisingly, seven
years later every one of them is still single.

Many people think falling in love should just happen. It
shouldn't be something we help to bring along.

I strongly disagree.

I think that a woman should consciously do everything in
her power to identify and then seek out the type of relationship
she desires. Setting the stage for the kind of love you want is
not artificial or unnatural. Unnatural behavior is continuing to
engage in casual encounters or remaining in a dead-end relationship because you believe that is all you deserve, that these
situations were meant to be, and that sometimes—if you're lucky—
love works that way. I believe there is no excuse for staying in
a relationship unless it is the best it can be for you and there is
every reason in the world for finding one that is.

Do you want to:

• Stop dreaming and take charge of your love life?

• Learn how to identify what you need and want from a
  man?

• Determine whether a particular man can satisfy you before
  you make an emotional investment in him?

• End dead-end relationships forever?

This book will help you. It will show you how to go about

listing the qualities you must have in a man. It will help you look more accurately at the man in your life, and at those you meet via the methods suggested here. This book will increase your romantic self-esteem and teach you how to control the path of your courtship from meeting to marriage.

Finding a mate is as serious a task as finding a job, yet many women cling to the notion that love is something best left to fate. They spend less time thinking seriously about what they want in a marriage partner than they do about what clothes to buy for work. Women who leave their romantic life totally to chance are acting from a position of weakness. Eventually, they will be acting out of desperation rather than from strength. Their behavior is self-defeating.

This book offers women the opportunity to start employing their most powerful resource, their minds, and to start operating in a way that always puts the odds in their favor. There is nothing neurotic or desperate about wanting to be loved by a man and to have a satisfying, nourishing relationship. All you need is a plan of action.

ROMANCE MANAGEMENT RULE #1:

Don't wait for love to "just happen." Go out and make it happen.

2

ROMANCE MANAGEMENT

You can't just sit there and wait for people to give you that golden dream: you've got to go out and make it happen for yourself.

—DIANA ROSS

IT SEEMS that we are expected to make most major decisions only after many of hours doing research. Remember how you had to write away for dozens of college catalogs before narrowing down your top choices? Or how your friends and family filled your ears with tips on distinguishing a great buy from a lemon before you bought that first car? Why is it, then, that we are so casual about our love life? I believe love is too important a part of one's life to entrust to mere chance and intuition. Without training to differentiate between sexual attraction and a sustainable emotional bond, it is impossible to choose between a man who is right and one who is wrong. Romance Management will provide you with all you need to know.

When I began to research the psychology of love, I realized how much practical use the theories could have in our everyday romantic life. I knew that if other women like myself knew about the theories and had specific strategies to follow in employing them, they'd be as eager as I was to put them to practical use. I decided to apply psychological principles to romance. I designed specific strategies for this purpose. When I applied the strategies, something clicked, and I knew I'd found the answer. Until now, I'd been acting directly counter to what is scientifically proven to work.

At first I worried that all my life I would have to use strategies. But gradually I discovered that the strategies helped me to present my real self. Men reacted positively to the sure, directed person my strategies had made possible. They knew that I knew what I wanted. And they knew that I respected myself too much to accept less. Knowing that I insisted on the best for myself may have even flattered their self-esteem.

The strategies enabled me to act in my own best interest. Before, dating had always made me feel self-conscious and insecure. Romance Management strategies allowed me to assume control of my love life. My approach became goal-directed and focused. When I next fell in love, I followed both my heart and the Romance Management approach right to the altar.

My women friends considered my new approach crazy until they saw the results I was getting. Soon they began to try these strategies themselves and enjoyed their new-found control. They became more discriminating and ultimately made better romance choices. My workshops evolved from my own successful use of the Romance Management approach. It has since helped many women achieve the happiness they so richly deserve.

What can Romance Management do for you?

- **Romance Management teaches you to act in your own best interest.**

  If you are like many women, you were brought up to believe that by putting your needs aside and being a good girl, someday you would be rewarded with a Prince Charming. As a result you have probably failed to act in your own best interest. While you would never hesitate to advise a close friend or relative to act in his or her own best interest, you falter when it comes to your own life. You're in a lot of good company. Romance Management is a way to take control of your love life rather than being a victim of it.

- **Romance Management places you in a position of power.**

  Having control in your love life is no different from having control over your weight, your career, or your temper. Control enhances your self-image and gives you the ability to affect your circumstances.
  Romance psychology puts men and women on an equal footing.

- **Romance Management lets you screen out inappropriate men.**

  Some men need to be single to be happy. That's their right. Don't argue with a man on the issue, and don't get involved with him. As challenging as such a man may seem, forget him! You don't want to waste your time on someone you have to convince to marry you. The smart approach is to find a man who may be interested in the idea himself. Through the Romance Management screening process, you will eliminate men who are not worth your effort.

- **Romance Management increases a man's desire, passion, and respect for you.**

  Many relationships end prematurely because the man fears commitment. By utilizing Romance Management, you will gently overcome his fears, enabling him to finally experience the joy of a loving relationship. Because you will be maintaining perspective and not over-romanticizing the relationship, he'll be more drawn to you and less likely to bolt.

You needn't feel guilty about using strategy. It is simply a way to act intelligently about your feelings so that both you and the man you love will find satisfaction with each other. Your man will be glad that you maintain his interest as well as anticipate and overcome his fears. Men want intimacy and closeness also, and Romance Management allows both of you to meet your needs.

One major difference between many men and women is their intimacy comfort level. Little boys are taught they must separate from their mother at an early age and establish their autonomy independently of her. Little girls, on the other hand, remain bonded to their mother, who later becomes their role model. When they grow up, women often seek to recreate the depth of the intimacy and closeness they felt in their first primary relationship.

As a result, men often need less intimacy in their relationships than women. Men tend to be drawn to uncertainty and challenge, while women tend to seek out security and stability.

You don't need to play a false game to infuse a new relationship with challenge and uncertainty to keep the man interested. But since you are going to pace your romance until you decide whether or not he can satisfy your needs, you'll naturally be offering him a challenge. When you're too easy to get, you fail to use good judgment because it doesn't give you time to decide if he's really right for you. And if you don't keep an initial distance and allow a degree of uncertainty, he will never convince himself that winning you is worth the effort.

In order to get to achieve your romantic goals, you must act in your own best interest. Ultimately this helps the man as well because the woman he wins is the woman he thinks she is. She is a woman who has clearly let him know what is essential to her in their relationship.

A word of warning. It's not enough to follow a diet for two months in order to lose weight, then slide back to your old eating habits. You must learn new dietary habits and incorporate them into your daily routine in order to maintain your weight loss. This requires that you practice will power and delay immediate gratification.

The same process applies to relationships. You can't expect long-term happiness in a relationship if you only practice Romance Management until you appear to win a man over. Acting in your own best interest should continue throughout your life. Not only must you learn new behaviors, but you must follow them consistently to obtain positive results. After all, learning to change your behavior is a small price to pay for eventually achieving your romantic goals.

Acting in your own best interest should become natural to you. It should not be something you do only on special occasions. It's tempting to revert to old ways of relating to men when things seem to be working out well. **THIS IS A MAJOR MISTAKE!** Abandoning Romance Management is similar to throwing out a business plan just as it makes you successful.

ROMANTIC GOALS

Successful enterprises require clear goals and methods. You must ask yourself first whether you are seeking a long-term or permanent relationship. If you are, what are you looking for in that relationship? Is it companionship? A sexy Saturday night date for life? Financial security? A family? The answer to that question can help clarify your objectives so that you become more focused. You'll also find that knowing what kind of relationship you want will change your attitude and behavior toward the men you will meet from now on.

Without a clear objective in mind, you will tend to date haphazardly and find yourself sidetracked into associations with men who are simply not right for you. By knowing exactly what it is you want in a man, you'll avoid unnecessary derailments.

This sounds like common sense, right? But when it comes to matters of the heart or sexual attraction, common sense is like the fire engine that arrives at a burning house after it is already reduced to a pile of ashes. Too often, we allow the caprice of physical attraction and charm, rather than our own defined objectives, to guide us in choosing romantic partners. In our desire for romance with a capital R, we let ourselves be swept away by intangibles like chemistry and enchantment. In the process, we overlook flaws and negative characteristics about our partner that must eventually destroy our fragile fantasies.

Following your objectives will not always lead to the best possible partner immediately. But by clarifying your goals, you can be certain that at any stage in your romantic life, whether you are presently seeking a relationship or are involved in one and hoping to move it toward a higher level of commitment, you will be acting in your own best interest. When you look out for yourself, you will bolster your self-confidence and self-esteem, and will always act from a position of strength and discrimination as opposed to one of weakness and desperation.

The following group of worksheets will help you formulate your romantic goals. You should make a copy of each one and fill it out as you read that section of the book. Later chapters build on the information about yourself that you will discover as you complete the worksheets. A second complete set of worksheets appears at the end of the book.

The Relationship Objectives Worksheet

The Relationship Objectives worksheet is designed to assist you in identifying your objectives and any obstacles that may stand in the way of achieving them.

Your Objectives

The first question asks for your relationship objective. Most women fall into one of the following romantic stages. You must

RELATIONSHIP OBJECTIVES

1. What is my relationship objective?

2. What is my time frame?

3. How high on my list of priorities is finding a mate?

4. What obstacles and roadblocks stand in my way?

5. What actions can I take to overcome these obstacles?

be honest with yourself and decide what stage you are presently in. First, you may feel very ready to marry. Or, you may not quite be ready and would prefer dating casually until an appropriate man comes into your life. Finally, you may feel ambivalent about men and relationships right now, and would like to take a break from dating.

READY AND WILLING

If finding a mate is your number-one life priority, there is an excellent chance you will reach your goal, especially if you follow the guidelines and approaches mapped out in this book. A ready, willing, and open attitude will serve you well as it will ultimately attract men who are as marriage-minded as you are.

The major pitfall, of course, is desperation. Just because you feel ready to meet and marry a partner for life doesn't necessarily mean that he'll appear tomorrow. So don't be tempted to appear at the door dressed in a wedding gown the next time you're asked out on a date! You still have to act in your own best interest, which means you must take the time to apply your standards of marriageability to every man you meet. Now, especially, you must not make any exceptions to the rule. If you do, you'll risk settling for the wrong partner and defeat your intentions in the long run.

COMPARISON SHOPPING

If you are in no particular hurry to settle down, you may want to date a variety of men. Canvassing the field is a good way to put together an inventory of qualities you'd like in a potential partner. When you approach casual dating with some discrimination, you may find that each successive man moves closer to the type of person who is right for you.

Jenny, a 32-year-old attorney, described what she learned from the process.

I realized after dating several men that if there was such a thing as a matrimonial blender, I'd be the first to buy one. In it, I'd put Jeff's sense of humor, Martin's even disposition, Frank's athletic build, and Steve's talent in the kitchen . . . and blend them all together. Out would pop my ideal man. Since I have to look for such a "blend" on my own without the help of such a fantasy appliance, I now realize I'm looking for a man with as many of those qualities as possible.

Comparison shopping presents one danger, however. It is very easy, if the man is attractive, for you to become ready and willing while he thinks you are both still shopping around.

Jeanette, a 28-year-old airline stewardess, met David, a successful businessman who often flew in her first-class section. She was aware of his past history, two marriages ending in divorce, yet she found him very attractive. When David eventually invited Jeanette on a dinner date, she accepted. Even though she had planned to keep things light, before she knew it, she fell in love. They became lovers, and soon Jeanette began pressing for a commitment. David made it clear he had no intentions of marrying again. Jeanette believed he would change his mind if she gave the relationship more time. The relationship dragged on for two years before she finally gave up.

Jeanette made two mistakes. First, she changed her agenda without considering thoughtfully whether David would actually fit her new game plan. Then, when she discovered he would not, she persisted in the relationship anyway. Rather than hoping to change David, Jeanette would have been better off looking for a new man.

Without a strong romance game plan behind you, casual dating can easily turn into casualty dating and prove costly in terms of time and emotional energy. If you ultimately want marriage, do you really need to look around as a way to get a sense of the kind of man you're after? Even if you haven't dated a great deal, in all likelihood you have some idea of the personality traits you desire. The next worksheet, entitled "My Ideal Mate," should assist you in clarifying what you want and help you avoid getting sidetracked with the wrong men.

TAKING A BREAK

Perhaps you've recently ended a painful relationship and are following your best instincts by not getting involved with anyone.

You need time to heal, regroup, and distance yourself from the experience. Perhaps you're in a period of transition and have neither the time or energy to devote to a new relationship. Or perhaps you have developed a negative view of your chances of ever finding a mate and have decided to forego dating for a while.

These are all legitimate reasons for putting your love life on hold. Give yourself permission to act and feel as you do, rather than feeling guilty or pressured to become romantically involved. This may be difficult if friends and family who are concerned about your emotional well-being encourage you to get involved with someone new, hoping it will make you feel better. As well-meaning as their advice may be, remember:

You are under no obligation to enter into a relationship to please anyone but yourself.

Until you feel ready again to pursue a relationship, seeking out new involvements is counterproductive. If you enter a relationship feeling ambivalent, you will consciously or unconsciously build an escape route from intimacy.

Your Time Frame

Knowing where you'd like to be romantically a year from now will assist you in planning how vigorously you would like to pursue your romantic goals.

Angie, a 36-year-old stockbroker, had this to say about her time frame.

> When I finally decided I would be ready to marry in two years, I found myself doing all kinds of things that anticipated the event. I bought my own home, furnished it, and began becoming more in tune with whether or not men had potential for me. I became more focused and am now seriously involved with a man I hope to marry. It has been about a year and a half since I narrowed my attention on the goal of finding a mate.

Some women use a time frame to limit the period they are willing to wait to see what their current partner's intentions are for the relationship. In other words, it helps to force the issue.

For Lauren, a 32-year-old commercial artist, the time frame helped her end a dead-end relationship just in time for something better.

> After being with Tim for two years, I got tired of his "not being ready," for a commitment. I finally gave myself a personal ultimatum of six more months in the relationship. I was 27 at the time and really wanted to settle down. It was hard to do, but when I didn't receive an engagement ring by the deadline I had set, I broke off the relationship. I resisted the urge to go back, even though Tom begged and pleaded. I'm glad I ended it because if I hadn't I wouldn't have met Dan. I was free and available when he came into my life and now I've found an emotionally mature man who wants the things I do.

Some women use a time frame as an incentive to motivate them to take action. If you have been saying you want a relationship "sometime in the future," establishing a time frame makes you think seriously about achieving your goal. However, setting a very short time frame will defeat your purpose. Allow a reasonable amount of time, eighteen months to two years, to meet someone and get to know him. Start now by forecasting a date in the future when you plan to marry.

Write that date here:_____

Mariam, an attractive, and goal-oriented motivational speaker, secretly set her wedding date twice before meeting the man she was to marry. The third time, she and her future husband set it together. She's convinced having an imaginary deadline, even though she extended it, spurred her on to meeting her mate.

Priority

How high on your list of priorities is finding a man to marry? Obviously this question applies to those women who are ready and willing. All the same, think about other demands on your time and attention, particularly career demands. Catherine, a 34-

year-old administrator for a home-health-care agency, described herself as ready for marriage but unwilling to sacrifice her career at this particular moment to take the time to date different men.

> A total reorganization of my company is taking place right now, so my main priority at the moment is to maintain my position at work and insure my future employment. I've set a goal of no longer than six months to continue putting in these 12-hour days. At that point it'll be safer for me to shift my priorities more from work to my personal life and spend the time required to meet more men.

Obstacles

Think about obstacles which may stand in your way. Some obstacles are self-imposed, such as the fear of entering a new relationship because you believe you are "jinxed" when it comes to love and any relationship you attempt will only end in disaster. Such an attitude can make you consciously or unconsciously present yourself in an unfavorable way to the men you meet, thus sabotaging the possibility of a relationship at the start.

Other obstacles are external, like not finding enough time to devote to a relationship. These require help in the form of time-management and problem-solving skills. You must recognize and overcome both self-imposed and external obstacles before moving forward in your quest.

One special internal obstacle is ambivalence. If you are not really ready to begin the search for a marriage partner, or fear intimacy for other reasons, you may do things which prevent true intimacy from developing.

Jill is a case in point. A 28-year-old graphic artist with her own company in San Francisco, her romantic life centered around long-distance affairs. When one of her lovers surprised her by accepting a transfer to San Francisco so they could be together, she became critical and demanding of him until they split up. Once the safe distance she placed between herself and true intimacy was removed, the relationship felt too close for comfort for her.

Diane, a 36-year-old management consultant for a major

corporation who had suffered through a painful divorce, had her own style of avoiding intimacy. She never allowed herself to get involved with an available man. Her relationships are with foreign exchange students, married men, and confirmed bachelors.

Ambivalence can also take the form of a relationship with a married man. A woman who is uncertain about becoming too intimate with a man may find that his marriage conveniently serves as a safeguard against the relationship growing beyond her emotional comfort zone.

You need to recognize the source of your unsure feelings as well as your right to have them. Work through these feelings and develop a game plan. Begin by completing the worksheets in this chapter. Focus your attention on what you want from a relationship and learn from past mistakes. This will make your future approach more clear-headed, put you back in control, and prevent you from becoming a victim of your past.

Recognizing Patterns from the Past

Looking at past involvements will alert you to your particular style of relating to men. Fill out the next two worksheets. They will help you see patterns you have already developed, some of which may be counter-productive. The first worksheet asks general questions about your attitudes and behavior. The second asks you to focus on the past three men in your life. This exercise will pinpoint what you do and don't want in a relationship and will help you recognize self-destructive patterns that sabotage your best efforts to establish a relationship.

Examine both the positive and the negative aspects of your last three meaningful relationships. The positive aspects will help you identify what virtues you admire and hope to find in an ideal mate. Even if you have difficulty believing you can benefit from the past and find it painful to recall the men you've been with, completing both worksheets will deter your repeating these mistakes. If you're over 30 and haven't been involved with many men because you married young or spent many years pursuing an education or career, don't skip this exercise because you think you haven't developed bad habits. You'll benefit from analyzing even one relationship.

RECOGNIZING PATTERNS

EXAMINING PAST EXPERIENCES WITH MEN

(1) Do your relationships evolve slowly or do you rush into them?

_____

(2) Do you tend to draw a false early impression of men and then feel let down when the truth comes out?

_____

(3) Do you always seem to give more in a relationship than you get?

_____

(4) When you enter into relationships are you willing to accept the men as they are, or are you hoping to make major changes?

_____

(5) How long have your last three relationships lasted? Who ended it?

_____

(6) Do you like the chase but get bored because the passion never lasts?

_____

(7) Are you attracted to unavailable, mean or indifferent men? Do you date exchange students or foreign men who are here on extended visas?

_____

(8) Do you feel men can't be trusted?

_____

(9) How do men fail to meet your needs?

_____

(10) Do you feel as if men don't want to commit to you?

_____

IDENTIFYING PATTERNS

EXAMINING PAST EXPERIENCES WITH MEN

	#1	#2	#3
1. Were you willing to accept him as he was, or were there any serious flaws? What were they? When were they first noticed?			
2. Was he available for a relationship?			
3. Were you?			
4. Did you marry, live together or date? For how long?			
5. Who pursued?			
6. What attracted you to him in the beginning?			
7. What attracted him to you in the beginning?			
8. Major disagreement?			
9. What was his biggest complaint about you? You of him?			
10. Who ended it?			
11. In what way did he fail to meet your needs? Do you blame him for the relationship failing?			
12. The quality you liked best about him. The worst?			

If you examine each relationship closely, you will recognize why each man appealed to you. You need to pinpoint what you hoped to gain from being with him, and what attracted you in the first place. In those romances that were basically healthy but didn't work out, recall the positive appeal the man had for you and what attributes you most admired in him.

Examine the relationships which were painful and destructive. Do you have a weakness for a certain kind of man who always does you wrong? Do some soul-searching and consider what clues or danger signals you can look out for next time.

The Attraction

Rethink the appeal the men in your past had for you. Was it lasting? Certain personality characteristics such as loyalty, trustworthiness, and a good sense of humor can be very appealing over the long run. Are you instead drawn to men with status? Do you hope to marry a man with money? If money is a criterion in addition to your most basic needs to be loved, cherished, and satisfied by a kind, considerate, and loving man, you're not the only one. High earning power attracts many women. But do not become an indentured servant no matter how large his bank balance is. Unless he is able to satisfy at least some of your emotional needs, you'll end up feeling like some other object he bought.

Whirlwind Romances

Being swept away may have led to many problems in the past. The chemistry of infatuation early in a romance clouds your ability to make sound judgments. When you rush into a relationship because it feels right, you don't allow yourself the time necessary to see the whole picture. You fall for a man precisely because you don't know him.

Surrendering to your emotions, going with the flow, resembles the experience of romance-novel heroines. Believing you're at the mercy of love and are following your heart rather than your head can release you from any responsibility for making the wrong choice. But the choice will still be wrong and you will suffer for it.

Is He Available?

Some women really like being the other woman. They do not seek men who can possibly become committed to them. Some women prefer a married man to no man at all. Such women are often discouraged by what they perceive as the lack of available men and succumb to the temptation to borrow or poach until they get one of their own.

Workplaces consistently and repeatedly expose women to married men. Added to this, women who have chosen to devote themselves totally to their careers often lack the emotional reserves required to nurture a full-fledged relationship. An affair with a married man provides a kind of convenient stopgap. It is preferable to being alone. Women frequently date a man knowing he is married.

Donna, a 35-year-old investment sales woman, describes her involvement with a married man and fellow worker.

Sam and I started out as friends and then he became my mentor. I was working 12-hour days and many of those hours we spent together going over investments or traveling around the state to service accounts. He saw I was lonely and had no private life. I confided in him and began to look forward to our conversations about my personal well-being and future in the company. He called me on the weekends just to see how I was. Eventually Sam began inviting me into his home for holiday dinners. The first time I met his wife, I began making comparisons and thinking how much younger, prettier, and more stimulating I was. I knew Sam was having the same thoughts, and soon our friendship grew into a full-fledged affair. But then the holiday invitations stopped coming, and the intimate conversations and weekend phone calls ended. Sam became more distant, rarely seeing me outside the office except to call me unexpectedly to sneak out and meet him at a nearby hotel. Sam continued to throw out crumbs to keep me hooked on my relationship with him and disinterested in the available men that wanted to date me. Luckily, a headhunter contacted me and offered me a higher paying job that took me out of the company and away from this situation.

For a single woman who is ambivalent about becoming too intimate with a man, a man's marriage serves as a safeguard against the relationship growing beyond her emotional comfort zone. The clandestine nature of the affair makes the relationship exciting. The couple share a separate reality, a little world of their own. What begins as a convenient arrangement, however, usually ends in pain and regret. Most women cannot compartmentalize their loving feelings into specific time slots. Moreover, an affair with a married man monopolizes your limited emotional capacity and keeps you too involved to seek out a more appropriate relationship.

Double Messages

When you get a double message from a man because his actions and words fail to mesh, you'll be tempted to listen to whichever message says what you want to hear.

When Joanne, a 32-year-old recently divorced photographer, began dating Ted, who was a few years younger and a criminal lawyer, she was swept off her feet by his constant attention and requests to see her every night. Though he had told her on their first date, and several times after, that he had no intentions of dating her monogamously, she believed his actions spoke louder than his words. After six weeks the intense physical attraction between them began to fade and Ted's words took on more meaning. He quit pursuing Joanne relentlessly and resumed dating others. When Joanne saw Ted in a neighborhood café with another woman, his words finally began to register. He really had meant what he said.

Duration of Relationships

Have you been able to sustain long-term relationships with men or do your relationships end abruptly before things really begin? You need to avoid mini-romances and pursue long-term involvements more conducive to a monogamous commitment leading to marriage. If you are always the one to break up with men, ask yourself why the men in your past failed to live up to your expectations.

Most of us have a problem acting in our own best interest when it comes to sexual and love relationships. Self-defeating problems plague both men and women. Once you become aware of your patterns, you can begin to change them through self-awareness or by consulting a therapist who specializes in this area.

Traps to Avoid

- "He will always be supportive of me in every way and act as my personal confidant, therapist, and best friend."

This is a lot to ask from anyone. Don't hope to find a man who will devote his life to satisfying your needs. You need to develop a network of people for support in times of trouble in time of trouble and not expect any one person to do all the emotional work.

- "When I meet the right man, my life will finally have some direction, some meaning."

You are the only person who can give your life meaning and direction. Act on this basic principal when approaching your love life in order to avoid unrealistic expectations about what a relationship can provide for you. Don't judge yourself or allow others to judge your worth on the basis of whether or not you have a mate. Until you develop a healthy acceptance of yourself, you'll be unable to attract the men you deserve. Therapy would be a wise investment if your self-esteem is suffering. It can change your outlook on life and improve much more than just your love life.

- "I can turn his life around."

Men who need to be rescued bring out the maternal instincts in women. Such men can need emotional and financial support as well as sexual healing. They can be addicted to drugs or alcohol. Perhaps they have never considered a job because it would be too "heavy." Just remember, your full-time job is often what he likes best about you. Forget this man. He is a human sponge. If you have an overwhelming urge to rescue the needy, do volunteer work.

My Ideal Mate and My Non-Negotiable Needs

When you go to the grocery store without a list and you are hungry, you may pick up all kinds of junk food you really don't want. You may even eat some of it while you cruise the aisles of the market, but your hunger won't be satisfied.

When you are emotionally hungry, you will choose men with this same junk-food mentality. With inappropriate men, however, you waste your love and emotional energy. In order to avoid choosing men on impulse and regretting it later, fill out the Ideal Mate worksheet and identify your non-negotiable needs.

This exercise encourages you to actually visualize what your ideal mate would look like and describe his most desirable characteristics. Unless you are able to identify and describe your mate in this manner, it is unlikely that you will recognize him if you meet. Visual imagery is quite powerful and your ability to describe the physical and spiritual image of your ideal mate will act as an unconscious incentive to finding him.

Physical Characteristics

Start by listing the physical characteristics you find most appealing in a man. Here you might include hair and eye color, height, and build. Men have always had their favorite "types"; you certainly have a right to a preference.

Personality Traits

Next, list the personality traits that you find most appealing. Draw on your memory of past relationships with men in order to recall which positive personality traits attract you most. You might include a sense of humor, emotional expressiveness, or honesty.

Beliefs, Values, Religion, Family

Most important, consider religion, age, basic beliefs and out-look on the world, values, politics, attitudes, and whether or not he wants or has children.

His children. It's important to be realistic about how his children will affect your lifestyle if you should marry. His devotion to his children is admirable, but there may be drawbacks. Are you willing to live with them? At first Amy, a 28-year-old actress, didn't mind the fact that David, a 34-year-old musician, had a 6-year-old daughter named Cynthia from a previous marriage. Amy thought David was a great father—just the kind of man she hoped to marry. Soon, however, Amy began feeling as if she were playing second fiddle to Cynthia. David would break dates at the last minute to be with Cynthia, indulge the child's every whim, and insist that she accompany the adults whenever they went away for the weekend. Amy understood that David was probably feeling guilty about his divorce and trying to compensate with Cynthia, but it didn't make her feel any better. She came to terms with the fact that she felt neglected in the relationship, and rather than playing the wicked stepmother role, she moved on.

Your children. If you have children, consider his relationship with them and his approach to childrearing. Is it similar to yours? If not, is he willing to compromise? Would he be willing to look the other way and allow you to raise your children as you prefer or would there be conflicts? Consider the same questions in regards to the way you'd relate to his children.

Also consider factors such as his educational level, career, and income. These areas are important to consider when projecting what your life would be like in the future. Don't overlook these areas just because they aren't "romantic" to think about.

Non-Negotiable Needs

You've drawn a sketchy profile of your ideal mate from which to work. Now list the areas in which you are unwilling to compromise. Some areas to think about include religion, political affiliation, whether to have children, a specific age range, a certain level of fitness, similar values, and emotional or financial stability.

The ability to be monogamous or to satisfy you sexually may be a priority for you. If so, list it. Draw on your memory of past relationships to recall areas of conflict which came as a result of an important need that was not satisfied. What was that need?

When my assistant, Danielle, a beautiful and outgoing 34-year-old woman in computer sales, began working with me part-time, she had been in a dead-end relationship with a man who never satisfied her needs. He was sexually selfish, argumentative, and critical of her looks, her career, and the way she was raising her son. But because she lived in San Francisco, where she thought there weren't many men to choose from, she believed she had to put up with the situation. On my urging, she designed a profile of her ideal mate and began fantasizing about him. One day she realized that a man she'd known for some time, but never thought of romantically, fit many of her qualifications. Because she focused on her needs and how to satisfy them, she is now happily engaged to the man she almost overlooked.

Once you set a goal, you are half-way to achieving it. But many women get sidetracked and lose sight of their goals. It's important to review them occasionally, especially when you meet a man who is totally tempting but totally wrong.

Elaine, a 35-year-old vice-president of a jewelry company, had mapped out her goals and filled out the Ideal Mate worksheet. She knew exactly what she wanted yet she came close to getting sidetracked.

Elaine told how Tim was the first man she'd met in a long time who really attracted her. They kept in touch and had lunch several times. He said he was miserably married and asked Elaine to spend a weekend with him as his guest in Palm Springs. She really wanted a weekend away and Tim said he wouldn't pressure her sexually, that he just wanted to enjoy her company. He also hinted that he might not stay married forever.

I pointed out that Elaine wasn't looking for a man who "might not stay married forever" to his current wife. She was looking for a man who was at this moment single and emotionally available for a relationship.

Elaine wondered whether she couldn't just go to Palm Springs for a good time, but I had to warn her that most women can't have a sexual fling and let it go. They usually yearn for more. After a lengthy discussion, we both agreed that she was flirting with a weekend diversion that wasn't "free" at all but potentially very expensive in terms of the emotional time and energy. Elaine now carries her Ideal Mate list in her purse and refers to it whenever she is tempted away from the path to her goal.

Eliminate the Non-Essentials

Are your expectations realistic? Examine your non-negotiable needs. Determine if you would compromise any of them. Is it really non-negotiable that he be the "right" astrological sign or have a specific hair color? The more non-negotiable your list of qualifications, the more difficult it will be to satisfy them all. Eliminate all but the essential ones. If your expectations are high, consider realistically assessing what you have to offer. In addition, if you have always felt self-conscious about some aspect of yourself, now is the time either to accept it and learn to love yourself as you are or else to take steps to improve or change it.

Gail, an attractive and fit 28-year-old aerobics instructor, had totally unrealistic expectations. She had, therefore, stayed in an eternal dating mode.

When she came to my workshop I noticed that she had to turn the page over in order to complete her list of non-negotiable needs. She was unwilling to compromise on astrological sign (cancer), birth order (middle child), hair color (blonde), career (in a helping profession), background (parents still married), past marital status (never married), and religion (Methodist). Gail's long list screened out many potential men. She really needed to become more realistic and drop a few of her requirements—for instance, birth order and astrological sign.

When you know what you want, you're more likely to get it. That's why taking the time to identify your non-negotiable needs is so essential. If you don't know what you want, you may end up with anyone and any kind of relationship—exactly what you have done so far in your life. Remember, your list of non-negotiables directs all future decisions you make about men and relationships. It is not unreasonable to expect 80 percent of your needs to be satisfied in a relationship. But you must know what they are.

Some women seem to attract men instinctively. They always seem to be in satisfying relationships. Yet they aren't any more attractive or successful than most of us. They simply seem to practice Romance Management instinctively.

Alice, a 38-year-old industrial engineer, explained it this way.

I think about myself and act in ways that enhance a man's image of me, while at the same time making me feel better about myself. I've never thought of it as "romance management," just self-care.

Margie, an outgoing 32-year-old police officer, said,

My friends are always asking how I attract as many men as I do. It's not that I'm any more attractive than they are, it's more how I orchestrate the relationship.

Passion is fueled by tension and uncertainty. Women commonly make the mistake of establishing too much certainty too soon by assuring the man immediately of their undying love and devotion. When a man has won a woman's heart too easily, contentment can soon turn to complacency. Many women ask how encouraging uncertainty can work if what they are seeking in a relationship is mutual commitment, emotional security, and stability. The answer lies in the fact that you can't skip from infatuation to long-term commitment in a short period of time, nor should you want to. Trying to establish certainty with a man early in a relationship will squelch the passion and romance. You'll be coming on too heavy and defeating your purpose. A man must *want* to commit to you, and in order for this to happen he must first want *you*.

SETTING LIMITS

The most important Romance Management technique is learning how to set limits. You set limits and maintain them because you have self-respect and you refuse to be treated in a shabby fashion. Ground rules formalize your courtship and remove you from the ranks of those who are dating casually. If a man turns out to have great potential, it is very difficult to move from casual to formal dating. If he has no potential, your set of standards will identify his inadequacies very quickly.

Let the men you date know your time is valuable and that you always plan ahead rather than leave things to chance. You can maintain a man's passion and interest long enough for the romance to amount to something more than a casual affair if you allow it to grow gradually. When you establish ground rules, you give the relationship time to do just that.

If you do not teach a man how to treat you, he may get into bad habits, one of which is casual dating. In casual dating a man asks you out at the last minute, almost as an afterthought. Initially, the spontaneity may seem exciting, especially if you have been sitting by the phone hoping for his call. Do Not Accept. Doing so sets the tone of the relationship as a casual one from the start.

Establishing limits and sticking to them will gain a man's respect. He will take you off his list of "casual" dates, and you can begin to build structure and permanence into your relationship. Your attitude also offers the challenge a man requires and it screens out men who are never going to treat you properly.

Why do men call at the last minute? Many men have learned to do this from past involvements with women who never let their needs be known out of fear of appearing too demanding. When a man senses there are no boundaries, he often takes advantage of the situation. Usually, however, he then loses respect for the woman, grows bored, and moves on.

You deserve to be treated with respect and consideration by a man, and it is your responsibility to insist upon such treatment. Otherwise you end up feeling angry and resentful over his behavior. In order to get the desired results, you must express your preferences clearly and firmly.

If you set no limits about how a man can ask you for a date, his behavior will often deteriorate to the point where he just drops by at any time of the day or night. This lack of consideration will carry over to other areas of your relationship. If you are accustomed to being treated badly, force yourself to set limits in an assertive and self-confident manner. At first this may be hard to do, but as you screen out the wrong men and gain respect from the right ones, it will become natural to you.

MY IDEAL MATE

MY IDEAL MATE WOULD HAVE THE FOLLOWING CHARACTERISTICS:

Physical characteristics

1. _____
2. _____
3. _____

4. _____
5. _____
6. _____

Personality traits

1. _____
2. _____
3. _____

4. _____
5. _____
6. _____

Hobbies/talents

1. _____
2. _____
3. _____

4. _____
5. _____
6. _____

My non-negotiable requirements in a mate

1. _____
2. _____
3. _____

4. _____
5. _____
6. _____

If you have especially low self-esteem and have a hard time being consistent and sticking to your ground rules, short-term therapy can often be very beneficial.

You need ground rules in other aspects of your relationship as well. Any man who believes he can call at the last minute, drop in unexpectedly, push you into having sex, or treat you like you're invisible whenever another woman is around is not worth your attention.

Establishing your ground rules and enforcing them consistently is necessary if you are to maintain your self-esteem as well as his respect and admiration.

Timing is essential. You must begin at the start of your relationship and expect his cooperation. Most men view inconsistency as weakness, and will continually test the rules, creating a power play between you. Once a man becomes accustomed to having his own way, he would rather leave you than relinquish his control.

If you have just begun dating and his offenses have been minor—such as showing up late for dates or calling at the last minute—you'll have little trouble backpedaling if you begin immediately. If you've been too distracted to notice, or if you really don't care if he is a little late, his tardiness may become habitual. This is how bad habits begin. Insist on proper treatment now, rather than letting his behavior slide until it becomes more neglectful. Don't wait!

Many women have asked me whether setting limits isn't self-defeating? Doesn't it just scare men off at the start and make them think you're a bitch? I say that rudeness lies not in setting standards, but in making someone wait. If a man thinks you're a bitch because you won't wait, you probably don't need him in your life. If you quit worrying about what he thinks and start being more concerned about how you feel, then he may too.

The right way to set limits is

• From the beginning

• Consistently

• In a calm and straightforward manner

- Without feeling guilty

The wrong way to set limits is

- Inconsistently
- Only in a crisis
- Hysterically
- While feeling guilty

ROMANCE MANAGEMENT TECHNIQUES

The following techniques are proven methods of Romance Management. The first two are especially helpful for setting ground rules in a nonthreatening way. These are the sweet and sour technique and mantalk.

Sweet and Sour Technique

The sweet and sour technique wraps a request around a compliment. The tone of your voice and general attitude are more important than what you actually say when using this proven technique. You want to act enthusiastic and upbeat.

If a man is in the habit of calling you at the last moment, the next time he calls, comment on what a great time you had the last time you got together. Next, let him know you would love to go out with him but unfortunately you have made other plans. Don't elaborate. Close by saying, "I would love to get together some other time."

If he is interested in you, you will undoubtedly hear from him again. Only the most insecure man will be put off by the possibility of your dating others. Most men will find you more attractive and desirable, knowing that other men are interested in you as well. And the next time he calls for a date, it will be with plenty of advance notice.

Dana, a 32-year-old physical therapist, used the sweet and sour approach with Steve, a 40-year-old chiropracter with whom she'd fallen into a casual dating situation. Dana had taught Steve he could drop in and out of her life. All he had to do was make a phone call and she'd run across town to meet him. At first being spontaneous seemed romantic. But eventually Dana seemed to spend most of her time waiting for his call. She felt "put on hold," especially when she'd leave a message and he wouldn't get back to her immediately. She would feel anxious and worried. Dana overlooked a basic Romance Management rule—she gave too much too soon and so was not getting much back. The relationship was unbalanced and there were early signs of relationship overexposure and burn-out. Steve had grown accustomed to getting his needs met whenever he was in the mood. Dana needed to establish some limits in the relationship because she had come to be in the weak position of feeling uncertain and out of control.

Even though she risked having Steve back off or even run away, Dana decided to take the necessary steps to regain a sense of herself. First she took a long drive out into the country. Once far away from her involvement, Dana realized her fears were out of proportion. She'd been in relationships before, loved and been loved by men other than Steve. If he wasn't willing to treat her the way she deserved, her life would not be over, she'd just find someone else. The following week Dana used the sweet and sour technique to soften the blow and motivate Steve to continue his pursuit while becoming more sensitive to her needs.

A conversation similar to this one took place when Steve called out of the blue one evening and asked Dana if she'd like to go to a movie that started in a half an hour and then get a bite to eat.

Steve: Hi honey, how are you?

Dana: I'm fine. But if you're calling to ask me to meet you, I can't.

Steve: How did you know I wasn't calling just to say hello?

Dana: You can never stand to just hear my voice. Once you do, you always want to see me. I just have that effect on men (using humor to break the ice).

Steve: So meet me in a half an hour and we'll go eat afterwards.

Dana: I'd like to see you too. I haven't stopped thinking about how great I always feel when I'm with you (sweet), but I'm busy tonight (sour).

Steve: You mean I'm going to have to start making "official" dates with you like we just met or something (snarling)? You know how my schedule is, Dana. I never know what I'm going to be doing.

Dana: I know what you mean about planning ahead. It is difficult (getting into agreement), but now I have other plans and guess I won't get to see you (holding firm).

Steve: Can't you change them? We haven't seen each other since last week.

Dana: I can't make it tonight (sour), but I'd love to make it some other time (sweet).

Steve had a hard time learning to break his habit of calling at the last minute, so the next time he called, Dana said, "Maybe we should make official plans to see each other (sour). Otherwise I'm afraid I may miss you again (sweet). Steve got the message that Dana was no longer available at the last minute so he modified his behavior and began planning ahead.

Dana felt so confident after setting limits with Steve that she promised herself she'd never give too much too soon in a relationship again. She saw clearly for the first time how important it was to act in her own best interest—for Steve's benefit as well as for herself. Otherwise she knew she would grow angry and resentful of the way he treated her and they'd eventually break up anyway.

Some women ask me if it isn't manipulative to use the sweet and sour technique to get results. Wouldn't it be better to be straightforward about your needs? It's great to be straightforward about your needs and I highly recommend it. When you use the sweet and sour technique, you're letting your needs be known directly and in a way that is most likely to produce results. Making a man more receptive to your requests is not manipulative, it's common sense.

Mantalk

Mantalk consists of short, concise talk, followed by action. It is the language men understand. You state what you want clearly and succinctly, and then you act in accordance with your words.

Consider this scenario. It's 3 a.m. You and your man have been involved in another marathon discussion, going around in circles for five hours, and he still doesn't appreciate your point of view. You're exhausted, frustrated, and angry, and you have to get up in four hours to go to work. You're no closer to a solution now than you were when the issue came up a month ago. You've lost so much sleep over it, you've been walking around with dark circles under your eyes and neglecting your work. The more you try to change his behavior, the more perversely resistant he becomes. What can you do?

You can speak to him in the language he understands and responds to. You can quit "discussing" your problems and start getting results. The language he understands is mantalk.

When a man asserts that another man is all talk and no action, he indicates a lack of respect for that person. Men feel the same way about women who complain endlessly about their needs not getting met. The more you "explain" yourself, the less credibility you will have with him. If he continues to be inconsiderate and you fail to take action, his respect for you will begin to wane.

Tess had explained herself repeatedly to Jeff about the way she felt when he invited his friends over to her place unannounced. Each time he did so, she explained her objections to him again. Though she got temporary relief by venting her anger, he kept showing up with friends and she kept whipping them up a last-minute dinner. Then she would spend the rest of the night complaining about it. Finally she learned mantalk. She quit explaining herself to Jeff. The next time he showed up with a party, she turned him and his friends away. She refused to allow him to make her feel guilty when he called the next day and declined his offer to come over and "talk" about it. Tess finally realized that rehashing the problem was a waste of time.

Many of us try to talk out our problems with men in the hope that they will listen and become sensitive to our needs. This is certainly the ideal, but usually when explaining your needs you should keep it short and to the point. When you go to great lengths, it only makes you look unsure of yourself. If a man fails to respect or meet your needs once you've let them be known, you must take action.

Unless you follow through with actions, a man will grow deaf to your words. Short, concise statements followed by actions will communicate more to your man than yelling, resentment, or all-night marathon discussions.

Acting the Way You Want to Feel

Acting more confident than you feel about a man's affection can pursuade him to share your point of view. Acting insecure can have the opposite effect. Because a man can't read your mind, he'll respond to the way you *act* rather than the way you *feel*, so the key is to act the way you *want to feel*. This isn't as complicated as it sounds.

Donna, a spokesperson for an airline, tells how she acted as if she were more confident than she felt.

I'm always nervous when interviewed in a moment of crisis. The way I conduct myself reflects upon the company I represent so I've learned how to project a cool, calm, articulate persona even when I don't feel that way. A few moments after I've got things under control, I'm no longer acting.

Actors, politicians, spokespeople, and talk-show hosts must "act as if" at least for a while until they actually feel more confident in a particular situation. Things are no different for you on a date in an unfamiliar situation with a stranger. Practice helps, which is why it's so important to date many men, so you can build up your confidence while perfecting your Romance Management approach. "Acting as if" doesn't mean you live in a fantasy world, or that you forget how to act in your best interests. It simply means that you consciously choose to assume, until proven otherwise, that the man you want appreciates you for who you are, is attracted to you, and, if all goes well, may fall in love with you. Your attitude may become contagious. It's a kind of mutual affection by osmosis. Our feelings about ourselves and the world around us influence others so creating within yourself a positive outlook on a romantic situation can cause it to move in that direction.

Acting more confident than you feel works because how people perceive you affects the way they treat you. Most women know that is true in their work life and with their friends as well. But what if it's impossible for you to act as if you're more confident than you feel because of strong negative beliefs you have about yourself? Or what if you've had so many negative experiences with men that you always carry around negative expectations that ultimately become self-fullfilling prophecies?

The following five steps to changing a belief, compiled by Virginia Ann Church, are based on the teachings of Dr. Maxie Maultsby Jr., a rational emotive therapist.

- Recognize what the belief is, and that you can change it.

Sandy, a well-dressed and attractive 32-year-old manager of a fashionable boutique in San Francisco, recognized she had a negative belief about her body image that held her back from getting romantically involved. Sandy ate healthy foods and loved outdoor sports such as tennis and hiking, but, according to the medical weight charts, was 20 pounds overweight. Though she longed to be in a loving relationship, Sandy believed that no man could ever love a women who was overweight. One day Sandy confided her belief to a co-worker, who persuaded her to come along that night to her women's group. There she met other women who weren't "model" thin but still managed to have lovers and husbands. One women in particular had a wonderful relationship with a man and an active and satisfying sexual relationship. She told Sandy she could too. This experience made Sandy believe she could change her belief and become involved with a man who would appreciate her as she was.

- You stop acting or thinking on the basis of the old belief.

Sandy began thinking more positively about her romantic possibilities after joining the group and meeting women who were overweight but didn't let that stop them from romantic involvement. She began noticing women on the street and in her shop who were even heavier than she was but who were accompanied by men who seemed to enjoy their company. She began adopting a more positive image of herself, thinking in terms of being "full-figured" rather than "fat" as she had in the past.

- You substitute a new, rational, and more personally meaningful belief for the old one.

Sandy replaced her belief that no man could love her with the belief that other women like her were in loving relationships and she could be too.

- You act in light of the new belief.

When a client offered Sandy two complimentary tickets to the premiere of a movie that everyone wanted to see, she acted on her new belief that she didn't have to be thin to be attractive. For months she had been admiring a man she'd met a few times, who managed a men's store down the street. One day she dropped by his shop and asked if he'd like to join her. He didn't hesitate to say yes. On their date, when he complimented her on her outfit, she didn't respond as she used to, by saying "this old thing?" Instead she just smiled and said thank you.

- You continue to behave in this rational new way, *even though it feels phony* to act this new way.

Sandy remained consistent in maintaining her new point of view. Three influences helped her in the process. Most important of all, her desire to change her outlook was strong. Second, her women's group, and specific members within it, reinforced her new belief. Third, her new, more hopeful attitude had the desired effect of making her appear more appealing and attractive to men who began asking her out. By changing her belief, Sandy found that there were men who found her full figure appealing and appreciated her just the way she was.

The bottom line is that by deciding you want to change a belief, taking steps to do so, and "acting as if," you reinforce the new and more positive belief until it becomes a reality.

Triggers

Triggers are ways of reminding a man who interests you that he has attracted your interest. Because the details of this technique are discussed in the chapters on Prospecting and Advanced Dating, I mention them here only because they are an important Romance Management tool.

Inconsistent Positive Reinforcement (IPR)

It is essential that you understand this all-important technique. It emerges out of a basic behavioral experiment with laboratory rats, but the pattern holds true for people as well. In the study rats learned to press a bar to get food pellets. Experimenters found that the rats worked harder and longer if they received a food pellet intermittently rather than every time they pressed the lever, or never at all. How does this apply to your relationship with men? Simply. If you offer all the love and affection like a love pellet to a man every time he requests it, he'll soon be satiated, just like the rat in the experiment that learns it doesn't have to work hard to win its reward.

If you've ever known a man who was interested in you, but whose affections you didn't return wholeheartedly, you've witnessed the powerful effects of an IPR schedule firsthand. Perhaps you went out with him once and weren't that interested. He would keep calling back and occasionally you offer him a little love pellet by going out with him again. Because you would throw out the little pellets inconsistently, he would keep coming back, working harder to win your affections.

Unfortunately, most women find it difficult to use IPR with men they care about. This is why they so frequently complain, of course, that only the men they don't want, want them. They just aren't able to apply the principal of IPR to men they want to keep. If you satiate a man you *do* like by consistently giving him whatever he wants, he no longer feels challenged to win you over and begins to take your relationship for granted. When this occurs, you frantically try to offer him more and more, even when he asks for nothing. As a result, both the man and the woman lose out. Overstuffed with "love pellets," the man becomes satiated, thereby losing the incentive and interest to actively demonstrate his loving feelings.

In order to prolong a man's interest and affection beyond the initial dating stages, it is necessary to avoid totally satisfying all of his sexual and emotional desires too soon. Being a giver goddess and offering yourself up unconditionally to a man before he's committed to you is one of the major errors women make when attempting to establish a relationship. When a women gives too much of herself too soon, most men will feel an obligation to reciprocate in some fashion whether they sincerely wish to or not. This often leads to resentment on the man's part and then his distancing himself from the relationship. For example, when a women sleeps with a man too soon and then expects more than a physical relationship, the man may feel obligated to show more affection towards her than he sincerely feels. After satisfying his sexual curiosity, resentment begins to set in and the distancing dance begins.

Predictably, this causes a switch in roles. The woman becomes the pursuer, and the man, uncomfortable with the level of intimacy, begins to back away. Hoping to draw him closer again, the woman offers a steady predictable diet of unconditional love. Just like the rat in the cage, without a challenge, the man begins to grow bored with the woman and lazy and uninterested in attracting her interest. He knows he has it all. The woman has achieved precisely the reverse of what she desired, and yet ironically she often believes that the relationship failed because she "didn't give enough." The opposite is nearly always true. She gave too much too soon.

At almost every workshop I have given, a woman will ask what happens if she uses inconsistent positive reinforcement on a man and it works. Will she always have to play a game with him? Will she ever be able to offer him all her love without holding back, and without his losing interest?

Once you've established a relationship with a man that is mutually satisfying and reciprocal, you should give freely. However, this doesn't mean that you should lose your sense of self or expect to satisfy all your needs through the relationship. Happily married couples know that even though they love each other, the relationship will go stale unless they work to infuse some passion and excitement into it. Women who worry too much about "keeping the peace" miss the point. A little fighting can help a couple let off steam and even add a little excitement and new-found closeness to their relationship. Relationships are not meant to always be smooth sailing. Remember, predictability is the kiss of death for any relationship. You need some uncertainty and excitement to stay interested. People in long-term relationships often tell me they think it's premeditated and unromantic to plan surprises, romantic getaways, or even sex dates with their lover. When I remind them of how much time and energy they spent during the early stages of their courtship, planning and scheming to sneak a little time away together, they agree that it didn't seem unromantic then, and it shouldn't now.

Don't think in terms of playing a game, but rather that you don't need to constantly offer a man your love and affection. Occasionally you should give him some distance from you so he can miss you, fantasize about you, and appreciate you more when you're not around. You need to have very special times together rather than a lot of just "okay" times together.

Nevertheless, the most important time to use IPR is during the initial stages of dating. It helps to prolong that first exciting passion. IPR is especially effective with men who are highly eligible and accustomed to having women chase after them. Never hope to win over such a man in the conventional manner. Highly eligible men are accustomed to having women anxious to date them. Why appear like all the others?

Begin employing IPR techniques during your first encounter. Forget the hard sell. Gather his interest and attention and then slowly withdraw from it. Never spend all your time in an attempt to win him over. It will leave you feeling as if you have been auditioning for a date all night. Don't offer him too much information about yourself too soon. Remain a little vague, reveal as little as possible. Maintain eye contact a little longer than you should and then ignore him for a little while. Let him come after you.

Once he asks you out, use IPR to hold his interest in you while you direct your energy toward gathering the information you need to determine his potential as a mate.

You don't need to be cruel when using IPR. You are simply trying to make the initial dating stages challenging so he will stay interested. If you satiate all of his desires right away, you do both him and yourself a disservice, for he will not come to appreciate you fully. Imagine being able to dine in an elegant restaurant every night and order your favorite meal. After a while you just wouldn't appreciate the experience as much as you did when it was an occasional treat you looked forward to. Allow your relationship to be special, something he looks forward to rather than something he "expects." You'll prolong the period of infatuation and offer the relationship a greater opportunity to move beyond the initial dating stages.

Here are some ways to offer inconsistent positive reinforcement.

- Don't always be available. If you are, he will assume he is your only social outlet.

- Don't always be affectionate. Be very affectionate sometimes; at other times let him initiate affectionate gestures.

- Don't always praise him and tell him how much you care. Do this occasionally, but no more often than he praises you.

- Don't always return his phone calls immediately. Let him anticipate hearing from you.

- Don't always cook his favorite meals. Do so occasionally and make it a special event rather than something he grows to expect.

- Don't always spend as much time with him as he would like you to. For instance, if he wants you to spend the whole weekend with him, only spend one day with him.

Self Care

Women have a tendency to become the emotional pursuers in relationships and men the emotional distancers. As a result, women may fall into the pattern of doing all the emotional work in the relationship, thereby allowing men to avoid expressing their thoughts and feelings. In order to break this vicious cycle and encourage a more equitable relationship, it is necessary for women to begin thinking in terms of self care and directing energy inward, towards themselves, rather than always outward in an effort to maintain the relationship. For many women this is a scary idea. They fear that if they don't do all the "work," the relationship may fall apart. Sadly, they are eager to criticize the idea of self care for this reason. Although it may sound like a game to intentionally withdraw some of your love and affection, continuing to play the role of pursuer while the man in your life seems indifferent will not win his heart or maintain your self-esteem. The key is to act on your own behalf, not out of anger at him, but in order to empower yourself and your relationship.

You begin by taking the focus and the pressure off the man. Break out of your pattern by seeking some satisfactions elsewhere. That may mean examining your life honestly and assessing whether or not you have been expecting too much from him. Seeking interests outside your relationship helps you remain a well-rounded person—whether you are in a relationship or not. Never put your life on hold for a man. If you've been waiting to meet someone before buying your own home, making a major career change, or going back to school, stop waiting. Do whatever you've been putting off. Meet a friend for a drink, take a course you've been wanting to, see a movie, attend a play, or go to a museum opening. When you're together with the man, have something to share and talk about other than your relationship. Soon you'll become less dependent on him for your needs. At that point you may decide all you've needed were outside interests, or you may find that you need a man who is more expressive. By directing energy into your own life, you will either balance the inequalities you felt in your relationship, or you may feel you need to move on. Either way, by employing self care, you'll feel more confident and ready to make changes. You won't be stuck in a relationship that doesn't satisfy your needs.

ROMANCE MANAGEMENT STRATEGIES

Let Him Pursue You

Let the man convince himself that you are the woman for him. Don't try to hard-sell yourself. Make it clear to him that you are interested, but let him do most of the pursuing. The effort and devotion a man expends in winning you will increase his conviction of your desirability. If he takes the time to romance you, the foundation for something more permanent will be established in the process.

Donna, a 42-year-old lawyer, says she gives a man plenty of encouragement but lets him pursue.

> I let a man know I'm interested and then wait to see what happens. If he's involved with someone else or not interested, I won't be hearing from him. If he's interested, he'll call and then I'll know the feeling is mutual.

Some women are willing to do more than just wait, but they still expect a little pursuing. They do not begin to chase. Tanya, a 39-year-old receptionist, occasionally asks men out, but after the first date she expects them to make the next move.

> Sometimes I'll ask a man to a party or dinner at a friend's house. If he doesn't start calling after that, it's over. He's either too passive, gay, or not interested, so why bother?

Maintain the Mystery

A man's curiosity acts as a strong aphrodisiac. It keeps him coming back for more and fantasizing about you when you're apart. It is a powerful and driving force that has the potential to move your relationship beyond the initial dating stages. Rather than whetting his curiosity, many women satisfy it prematurely. When you do this, you remove the incentive a man needs to pursue getting to know you.

Many women dash into total disclosure, hoping for instant intimacy and unconditional acceptance. They rush to fill in the unexplored areas of their lives, to share all, to merge totally with the new man. They eagerly surrender to his pursuit and remove all obstacles from his path. They fail to realize that a man is drawn to what he has to discover, not what he already knows.

Stress Similarities, Not Differences

Since we tend to feel more comfortable around people like ourselves, it's important in a relationship to concentrate on your similarities, especially at the beginning. When he sees that you share many things in common, he will be more open to accepting the differences which are bound to come up as time goes by. Spend quality time discussing and participating in things that you both enjoy so that you can establish a bond beyond sexual attraction that will make you stand out as someone more than just a casual date. Be creative. Plan get-togethers that involve active involvement in your common interests, such as going sailing, seeing a play, playing tennis, visiting a museum. If he has an interest in an area you know little about, tell him you're curious and let him teach you something about it. He'll enjoy being the expert. Even if he turns out not to be the one for you, you will have added another topic to the variety of subjects you can talk about with someone else.

Activities other than having dinner and attending movies will give you an opportunity to see him from different angles. You can better assess his personality and how he deals with other people and social situations.

Backpedal, When Necessary

Sometimes you must be willing to risk losing a relationship in order to regain some control. If you deserve better treatment, you've nothing to lose by risking the relationship and everything to gain. The longer you procrastinate, the more firmly set in his ways and resistant to change he becomes. Also, the emotional stakes grow as you become more involved with him and less inclined to risk losing him to get what you want. Never bluff, then back down and expect things to change.

If you've been involved for some time and his habits are deeply ingrained, backpedaling is still possible but will require more effort and determination. You'll also have to endure a period of discomfort and uncertainty as he rebels and tests your resolve. If he fails to comply, you must be willing to relinquish the relationship and move on. Remember, if you back down, you will be settling for the wrong man.

As a first step in backpedaling, change the way you relate to your man. Your former approach has not been getting results. If you have been screaming and yelling, you may feel better temporarily but it does no good in the long run if he doesn't improve. You feel like a shrew and he'll be justified in distancing himself from you. If you've been pretending his inconsiderate behavior doesn't bother you, he'll keep it right up since you don't follow your words with actions. Indeed, as your resentment and anger escalate, one day you may erupt inappropriately at some minor offense and place the relationship in crisis. The longer you wait to correct a problem, the worse it gets. You must either quit complaining and accept the situation as it is, or else take action immediately to improve it. If you do not receive respect in your primary relationship, your own self-respect will eventually erode.

Sam, a 42-year-old accountant, had been calling all the shots in his relationship with Kathy, a 38-year-old hairdresser. He would drift in and out of her life, not calling for weeks, and would then expect her to drop everything in her life to see him. Sam determined the length and frequency of their dates, knowing he could spend the night, the weekend, or the rest of his life with Kathy if he chose to. He knew she'd take whatever she could get. But that was before Kathy and I started working together.

Kathy began setting limits on the amount of time she allotted Sam. She began giving him less than he was accustomed to. If Sam wanted to spend the weekend together, she would only spend half of it with him. If he wanted to go away together for a few days, she'd go for a day and a half. Kathy kept her schedule busy, so plans had to be made ahead. This made it more difficult for Sam to disappear from her life and then drift back into it.

Finally Sam began to realize he might be losing her. It was hard for him to face his fear of intimacy, but since Kathy wouldn't allow him to waltz in and out of her life whenever he chose, he realized he'd either have to deal with his fears and show more consideration or else start over with someone new who wouldn't expect as much from him.

Limiting the amount of time she spent with Sam was difficult because it was the exact opposite of what Kathy wanted to do. She was afraid that if she started pulling away from Sam, he wouldn't come after her, but would simply find someone else more accommodating. After we discussed it, Kathy decided she was willing to take that risk. She'd rather backpedal and have more control over her love life with Sam. If he left, she would rather move on. This new attitude showed Kathy was practicing self care. She was placing her needs for emotional stability and well-being high in her list of concerns. She was able to weather the rough times with Sam, knowing how he was, loving him despite it, but not allowing herself to become a victim as a result of it.

Diane, a 36-year-old physical therapist, had slipped into the habit of letting Larry, her new 34-year-old business executive boyfriend, get away with making snide remarks about her in front of friends. Diane couldn't figure Larry out because he was always so nice when they were alone. He convinced her she was imagining things or too sensitive about what he called "teasing." She didn't want to overreact. After all, it had been so long since she'd met anyone she wanted to date, much less sleep with, that she didn't want to make a fuss. One night at a party a friend followed her into the ladies room and asked her point blank, "Why do you let him talk to you like that? It's embarrassing to watch!" After doing some soul-searching and comparing notes with friends, Diane realized she had some legitimate concerns and needed to act on them immediately. During an emergency consultation, I helped her come up with the following plan to backpedal and try to regain some control in the relationship.

Since Diane had already spoken to Larry about his putdowns and hadn't gotten any results, we decided that they should have another discussion. This time Diane would tell Larry that there would be some negative consequences if he were to continue this behavior. Diane used the sweet and sour technique and mantalk with Larry to get results.

Diane: Larry, there's something I want to talk about that's really been bothering me.

Larry: What is it?

Diane: I believe your idea of teasing and mine are different. To me it always feels like a put-down.

Larry: You're acting sensitive again.

Diane: I can understand how you might think I'm being sensitive because we have different opinions about a lot of things and that's what attracted us in the beginning (sweet). But now, the fact we are so different is causing a problem (sour). Our definitions about what teasing means are different. If you put me down in front of friends again, I'm going to walk out on you (mantalk).

Larry: Can't we talk about this some more?

Diane: I'd be happy to talk about it some more (sweet), but talking more isn't going to change my mind (sour). I won't tolerate your put-downs anymore (mantalk).

Larry's habit of putting Diane down was hard to break, but Diane thought Larry had some promise as a mate, so she gave him a second chance. On their very next evening out at another couple's home for dinner, Larry made a joke about how Diane had forgotten to balance her checkbook and had bounced a $50 check. Diane had anticipated another put-down like this and had arranged to have her own transportation handy. As soon as Larry had shared Diane's most recent mishap with the party, Diane calmly stood up, excused herself, and walked out (mantalk). Finally, Larry was having to experience some discomfort and embarrassment because of his inconsiderate behavior.

Larry was surprised how matter of fact Diane was when they discussed the incident when he finally got through to her on the phone a week later.

Larry: I can't believe you walked out on me in the middle of dinner! And you haven't returned my calls in a week. What is wrong with you?

Diane: Larry, dinner was delicious, and I'm sorry I didn't get a chance to finish it (sweet), but I really lost my appetite after you began putting me down. I told you I'd walk out on you if you did that again and I meant it (sour). Do you have a bad memory (humor)?

Larry: No, I remembered, but it just came out. Give me another chance.

Diane: I'll think about it.

Diane did give Larry another chance but he couldn't change

his personality. Wisely, Diane moved on. By using the Romance Management strategies as a screening process to find out quickly whether he would change, Diane got the answer she needed and could make her decision.

Sex Too Soon

Sexual backpedaling is particularly important. When a relationship becomes physical prematurely, it often remains physical in the man's mind. It doesn't grow beyond a sexual encounter. In addition, sleeping with a man too soon causes many women to lose perspective. They begin over-romanticizing the relationship before it even gets off the ground. The man, however, may simply consider it a sexual conquest. Before sleeping with a man you must develop an emotional bond. If he's made an emotional investment with you, he'll be less likely to bolt the morning after.

Many men will test you to see how far you will go because men are more comfortable when they know where you stand on the sexual issue. It is the uncertainty that makes them feel they should push for sex. Once you let a man know you're not interested in casual sex, he will either respect your feelings and stick around long enough to earn your trust or move on. Don't give in out of a fear of losing him. If you sleep with a man too soon, you'll most likely lose him anyway. Moreover, you'll feel used in the process because you opened up to intimacy and were quickly rejected.

Joanne, an attractive 31-year-old real estate broker, had slept with Phil, an attorney she was wild about, on their first date. She hadn't heard from him since. After ten days her self-esteem was suffering badly. Since the date she realized she'd made a serious mistake. Phil was extremely attractive and eligible and now she was in grave danger of becoming just another conquest. If she ever heard from him again, she wanted to backpedal and salvage the relationship if it could become more than a purely physical one.

We devised a plan. Two weeks after their first date, Phil made contact. He mumbled some excuse about being busy with work. Joanne made no comment and agreed to go out the next week. After a lovely dinner they returned to Phil's place for a nightcap. He made a sexual overture, at which time Joanne smiled sweetly and said, "Phil, I really don't think its such a good idea that we sleep together (sour). I really like you a lot and enjoy your company (sweet), but I'm not comfortable getting sexually involved with a man I see irregularly."

Phil was shocked at her response. Rather than hanging around and teasing him, Joanne said good night and left (mantalk). Phil called a few days later and they began dating on a more regular basis before sleeping together again. Although Joanne had to risk losing the relationship in order to get what she needed, she now had a chance for a real relationship.

Maintain Perspective

It is essential that you maintain perspective while dating. Do not over-romanticize your relationship or develop unrealistic expectations about a man you hardly know. You need to remain clear-headed to prevent yourself from editing out valuable information about him.

When you are dating only one man, it is easy to focus too much on the relationship. Being too concerned about his opinion of you will make you come across as too intense. You need to strike a balance between making a good impression and realizing that he is not the last man you will ever meet. If you have been out of circulation a long time, you have no one to compare him with, and may quickly lose your ability to maintain good judgment. Work to overcome this.

Learn to keep your options open and not put everything else in your life on hold when you meet a man you think is right. If you are worrying about where the relationship is headed, he'll sense your urgency. One way to maintain your perspective is to date more than one man at a time, even if you aren't interested in sleeping with them. An involvement with others will make you less vulnerable and help you lighten up. Dating is a numbers game and you are much better off with a few men to choose from rather than pinning all your hopes on the first one that comes along.

If you're having a hard time meeting other men or wish to date only one man at a time, pace yourself. Avoid spending all of your free time with one man. You must not drop everything else in your life. Maintain your other friendships with both men and women so that you have other interests and engagements besides waiting for your next date with him.

Betsy describes how she failed to maintain perspective in her past relationships.

> Whenever a man was interested in me, and the feeling was mutual, I immediately expressed all my loving thoughts and feelings towards him, began planning to spend the upcoming holidays together, and started imagining how our child would look.
>
> I'd call him at the office just to say I was thinking of him, rearrange my schedule so I could sit at home in case he might call, and send sentimental cards. Soon he began backing off and I'd feel rejected. Finally I began maintaining perspective and became more discriminating. I quit falling for every guy on the first date and acting so needy. Whenever I start to get that way again I practice "non-needy" behaviors and start feeling more in control again.

Clinging Vine Syndrome

Are you a clinging vine? Men are not attracted to needy women. If you act needy, you may be sabotaging your relationships without knowing it. You can learn ways to keep your neediness in check which will not only make you appear more appealing to men but will also build your self-confidence. The following questions will help determine if you should act less needy.

- Do you latch on to a man at a party, monopolize him, and practically have to be pried away?

- Do you interpret everything a man says to fit your needs rather than reality? Do you over-romanticize the relationship?

- Do you plan your weekends only after hearing from him, even if that means waiting until Friday evening?

- Do you break dates with friends when a man calls at the last minute?

- Do you stay glued to your man's side, vigilant as a guard dog to any possible threat to the relationship?

- Do you call him late at night for "no reason" or constantly check your answering machine to see if he called?

- Do you constantly ask for reassurance from him? Do you always ask, "Do you love me?" or "Why do you love me?"

- Do you always say you love him before he says he loves you?

- Do you hang around the morning after like a devoted puppy, hoping your master will ask you to stay?

- Do you call him up to see if he is home and then hang up when he answers?

- Do you park outside of his house just to be near him, or to see what he's up to?

- Do you let men abuse you verbally and physically?

If you do any of these things, you should recognize your behavior. All of them describe clinging vine tendencies, and some show seriously low self-esteem. We all experience phases of insecurity, of course, and those moments can be the foundation of clinging behavior.

Look back to the Patterns worksheets you filled out earlier in this chapter. Especially examine your actual past relationships. Have you acted needy in the past? If the answer is yes, you may not just be going through a brief phase of insecurity due to recent events (breakup of love affair, loss of job, another birthday). You may have a full-blown case of clinging vine syndrome, which is devastating to most relationships. What can you do?

- Short-term therapy with a professional or even intense introspection can help you discover and deal with the source of your insecurity.

- Positive role models can help you learn new, more effective ways of dealing with men.

- Acting confident can gradually make you feel confident deep inside.

- Pursuing an interest you really enjoy will give you something important in your life besides a relationship.

Rachel, an outgoing and successful 38-year-old interior decorator, was confident and charming when working with her clients but felt like a nervous 12-year-old whenever she was around a man she was attracted to. She had been divorced for two years and was finally ready to meet someone new, but the prospect of meeting new men made her anxious. She desperately wanted to enter into a relationship, and consequently exhibited many of the behaviors listed above. In particular she constantly asked for reassurance and she allowed men to abuse her. She knew her behavior sabotaged relationships with the men she was attracted to and attracted men who only reinforced her low self-esteem. When she came to me, I first referred her to a therapist so she could begin working on the source of her problems. In conjunction with her therapy, we began working on ways to change the unattractive and unhealthy needy behavior.

I encouraged Rachel to think of women she knew whom she admired (role models). She mentioned two friends who acted self-assured when around men and she began to examine and copy their behavior. Here are some of the things Rachel learned from her role models.

- Confident women don't feel they need to convince a man they deserve him.

- Confident women assess whether or not a man is worthy of them rather than letting the man determine whether the woman is worthy.

- Confident women don't monopolize men. They assess his interest in them and move on quickly if their interest is not reciprocated.

- Confident women never date a man at his convenience; they require that he be considerate enough to call ahead.

- Confident women don't always try to please the men in their lives. They have a healthy concern for their own well-being.

- Confident women don't hide their needs, nor are they always cheerful with men.

- Confident women don't overanalyze situations and they don't second guess. If they are unsure about what is going on, they ask.

- Confident women are not watchdogs of their relationship. Believing in themselves, they don't feel they have to "protect" their man from the competition.

- Confident women never tolerate abuse from men.

Robin's best friend, Jennifer, is a needy woman. Robin and Jennifer have been on the outs because Jennifer cancels plans with Robin at the last minute whenever Steven calls. One Sunday when Robin and Jennifer had tickets to go to a special museum showing they had both been looking forward to, Steven called, so Jennifer cancelled again, leaving Robin in the lurch. Robin was hurt and angry that Jennifer didn't show any consideration for her feelings. Robin declared that it was always that way when Jennifer got involved with someone. She would put their friendship on hold, yet expected Robin to be around to offer support and encouragement when the romance fell apart. After the museum episode Robin decided she wouldn't be there any more because she wanted a full-time friendship not a part-time one.

Jennifer is in danger of losing her best friend as well as her support system if her romance doesn't work out. Her behavior is short-sighted and self-destructive.

Dropping everything whenever you meet a man you like is a warning sign that you are losing perspective. Remember, a man should enhance your life rather than be the center of it.

ROMANCE MANAGEMENT DON'TS

Don't Provide Total Accountability

Never freely account for your evenings away from a man during the early stages of a relationship and do not provide total accountability of your time to any man who has not given you a commitment. If you give out this information too freely and too early, you appear too accommodating and available. The man becomes too sure of himself and less motivated to win you over. Why should he, when he knows you're at home waiting? No woman would dream of telling a prospective employer that she was considering that job only, yet many young women are eager to assure a new man that other men mean nothing to her, that they are "just friends." This is a major error in logic. Why let a man know the coast is clear? Men thrive on competition. Once you let him know there is none, he's likely to feel more pressure than passion. Instead, allow for some doubt in his mind until you are getting closer to a commitment and he has earned the right to be certain.

Fay, a 34-year-old interior designer, was excited about going out with Arthur, a 42-year-old architect. On their first date she talked about how difficult it was to find men to date in San Francisco who weren't married or gay and that he was the first man she'd been out with in a long time. Fay's "true confession" made her sound like a helpless victim and Arthur felt pressured to "rescue her." Though there had been a strong initial attraction, Arthur backed off quickly and began calling infrequently, once every two or three weeks. Fay would get her hopes up but Arthur kept his distance because he thought Fay was desperate. Being too accountable had precisely the opposite effect of what Fay intended. Instead of bringing Arthur closer to her, it scared him off.

Don't Feather His Nest

Although it's thoughtful for you to demonstrate you care by occasionally cooking a man's favorite food or treating him to the theater, don't go overboard. Don't get into the habit of always cooking or cleaning for him. He'll begin to take you for granted and expect you to perform these duties regularly. If he is a slob, suggest he hire a maid. If he needs a secretary, offer him the name of a good employment agency. Unless he is willing to return the favor, never diminish yourself to the role of domestic or girl Friday.

Don't Be Instantly Available

You're not instant coffee so don't be instantly available. A man should not be able to walk in and out of your life at will. You are not a fast food outlet. If he wants to see you, he must show some consideration for the fact that you have a life as well.

Don't Let Him Stake Out His Territory

David was always leaving something behind at Tracy's. It worked like a warning signal to other men she dated that he had already established squatter's rights. When Tracy realized this, she sweetly handed over a bundle of his things, telling David her closet was already overstuffed with her own things and she couldn't accommodate his as well. Tracy was no longer willing to put his possessions or the relationship in storage.

Don't Phone Date

Some men use lengthy phone calls as a way to get emotionally recharged and then they disappear again. Keep conversations short and pleasant. If a man wants to connect with you, he will have to make a date.

Tracy placed a clock by the phone and followed a policy of never staying on longer than ten minutes. On a pad in front of her she had lists of things she could be doing instead of talking. As she was getting off the phone, she'd refer to a new excuse, checking it off as she used it "I have to see a client," "I have paperwork to do," "I'm meeting a friend for lunch." Tracy stopped neglecting other areas of her life in order to participate in phone sessions with David, which satisfied his needs and none of hers. She began getting more work done and feeling less used. David realized that he'd have to arrange an appointment to talk with her. He began asking her when a better time would be for him to call so they could "really" talk. Tracy said, "Over dinner would be nice." David got the message and asked her out.

Don't Play Mother or Therapist

Don't slip into the habit of working out all of his problems for him, fussing when he doesn't finish his vegetables, or com-

plaining that he's not living up to his "full potential." If he needs
therapy, he needs to seek it out himself or it won't be as meaningful or beneficial for him. Never send a man to a therapist to
convince him he needs to commit to you. It may backfire and
have the opposite effect.

Don't Play Hard to Get, Be Hard to Get

Romance Management is not a few principles you memorize
and put into effect just long enough to snare the man of your
dreams. It is an attitude and an outlook you carry with you always
to assure that you act in your own best romantic interests whether
you are on your first date or celebrating your twentieth anniversary.

ROMANCE MANAGEMENT RULE #2:

*You must practice Romance Management consistently and over
a long course of time in order to get permanent results.*

3

PROSPECTING
FOR LOVE

Too much of a good thing is wonderful.

—MAE WEST

WOMEN are always telling me how lucky I am when they meet my husband, Neal. But luck didn't bring us together—the ad I placed in a local newspaper's personals section did. I manufactured my own luck by advertising. It wasn't fate that brought us together, but a conscious investment of time and energy, plus application of some basic marketing strategies. Now of course everyone knows placing a personals ad isn't romantic. Accidentally meeting is. But you can't depend on chance encounters happening. You need to plan on meeting the right man not by accident, but on purpose, by taking steps to manufacture your own luck. Your first step occurs when you give yourself permission to have the type of relationship you deserve—a good one.

A SENSE OF ENTITLEMENT

Women who feel entitled to good relationships are the ones most likely to have them. Why? Because our attitude plays a big role in determining the kind of relationship we get. It's almost a self-fulfilling prophesy: what we expect and anticipate will happen.

Women who feel good about themselves radiate a powerful message. Men are far more attracted to them than to women who lack self-confidence. Confident, entitled women are more likely to let their needs be known in a relationship, stick by sensible ground rules, and earn men's respect and admiration. Many women don't believe they have the right to choose the kind of man they want. They wait to be chosen and they get whatever happens to come along. If you are able to give yourself permission to act in your own best interest without feeling guilty about it, you can start having the type of relationship you deserve.

We all know women who convince not only the men in their lives but everyone else as well of their desirability. They do this because they are convinced of it themselves. Often they are not exceptionally talented or attractive, yet they have no problem getting married. How do they do it? By believing they are entitled to a good relationship and acting in ways that reinforce that notion in the minds of the men in their lives.

If you feel you always attract losers, you should work to increase your self-esteem. Since you will probably continue to attract inappropriate men in your present state, it may be best to put your pursuit of a partner on hold for a while. Work on the areas that will improve your self-confidence. You'll be surprised how making even one small change will make you like yourself better almost instantly.

Betty, a 41-year-old librarian, felt so self-conscious about her thick southern accent that she rarely spoke unless she had to. She decided to take an adult education course offered by a speech therapist. She lost some of her accent, increased her self-confidence, and began taking more risks. While she has yet to meet someone special, she's more self-confident and open to the likelihood of it happening than she was a year ago.

Although a sense of entitlement is all-important, it's not enough just to *think* you want to meet the right man. You must *do* something to make it happen. You might have to meet one or two hundred men before finding a compatible match. In order for this to occur, you have to develop a plan of action to increase your exposure to men. In other words, you have to prospect for a mate!

DEVELOPING A PLAN OF ACTION

To meet men you must plan ahead to make it happen. Start the process now by filling out the Plan of Action worksheet.

The first question on the Plan of Action worksheet asks how many hours a week you will commit to finding a relationship. The time you commit will vary depending on how busy you are, but try to incorporate some activity into your schedule each week. This may take the form of attending a cocktail party given by a professional organization or going out for breakfast at a neighborhood café. (Bachelors are confirmed breakfast eaters and prefer their morning meals out.) If you haven't got much time to prospect, consider personals ads, video dating, or matchmaking. All three are very time-efficient.

PLAN OF ACTION

---

1. How many hours a week am I committed to finding a relationship?

---

2. Have I ended dead-end relationships?

---

3. Do I have a support person in my life?

---

4. What new groups or organizations am I willing to join?

Question two asks if you have truly ended your emotional involvement in any dead-end relationships. Officially you may not be seeing an old boyfriend, but if you're still pining for him, and secretly hoping you'll get back together, the relationship is not yet over—you're still in it, albeit alone. Carrying a torch for another man won't make you feel as open as you should be toward the possibility of meeting someone new. If you are still involved, summon up the courage to move on. Put the old relationship out of your mind once and for all. If you need to obsess about someone, start thinking about the man you'll soon meet who'll be so much more satisfying than the last one. After all, there *is* a reason why you no longer see the old one.

If you are keeping a man in reserve until "something better comes along," remember, the longer you hold on to such a relationship, the weaker your incentive becomes for attempting to find a new relationship.

The third question asks if you have a support buddy in your life. Before you begin prospecting, surround yourself with the kind of support you need. You need someone to share your plans with and solicit feedback from. You need someone to encourage you when you're feeling down. Some women choose just one friend, while others surround themselves with several positive, cheerful people who can support them in their quest to find a mate.

The last question asks what new groups or organizations you can join. Put together a list of possibilities and start investigating those that would be right for you. Don't forget to consider the group's gender makeup. Make sure it has a favorable ratio of men to women.

SEEK AND FIND

Where are all the men? From the numbers of single women who ask me this question you'd think that only Scotland Yard could find them. But before we dispatch the detectives, I have good news. Men are everywhere! It's not even a matter of selecting one specific place over another that's important (although certain public places have a greater ratio of men to women). What really affects the likelihood of your meeting someone when you're out is your attitude.

Have you ever asked yourself, "How approachable am I?" If you have a friendly, open face and a curious disposition, you can meet men anywhere. No matter how beautifully a woman is dressed or how elegant her surroundings, if she is wearing a negative attitude, those around her will notice and stay out of her way. Each time you head out in public, make a conscious effort to wear a friendly, approachable expression. Consider your outlook and behavior to be as important a part of your outfit as your clothes. Ask a close friend whom you trust to tell you the honest truth about how you come across when socializing. If you're not acting friendly and approachable, ask yourself why. Maybe you're feeling a little shy or insecure. If this is the case, begin by placing yourself in situations where you are most likely to feel more comfortable and at ease, such as at small get-togethers or in a class where the focus is off you and on an interesting topic. Entertaining at home is a great way to build up your confidence and showcase your talents as a gracious hostess, and you needn't invite dozens of people. Start off with a small group for drinks or coffee and dessert and then work up to a dinner party. Entertaining at home pays off with invitations from others and offers you the chance to polish your social skills. In addition, if there is a man you've been wanting to get a closer look at, a small get-together is the perfect chance for you to get to know him better.

If your lack of approachability has more to do with your negative attitude about men than feeling shy or awkward, you may need to examine your general beliefs about men and decide whether or not you can change them. If you project your feelings of disappointment and negative expectations upon every new man you meet, chances are your beliefs about each new man will become a self-fulfilling prophecy. Short-term therapy may be what you need to overcome this obstacle.

Where the Boys Are

Sports Activities

Whether spectator or participatory, sports always attract a greater number of men than women. You needn't feel intimidated about attending if you're not exactly the jock type yourself. It can make a difference, however, to brush up on the terminology of the sport. Just reading a program at a spectator sports event will fill you in on the names, positions, and statistics to date of the players. You'll be surprised just how useful it is to know even this much when striking up a conversation with your neighbor as the game progresses. Chances are any man you get to know will never figure out that your real intention when you came to the game had nothing to do with the team's World Series chances.

Here's a list of sports activities with a favorable ratio of men to women:

Basketball Games
Baseball Games
Bike Riding (especially organized rides)
Car Racing
Fly Fishing
Golf Tournaments
Horseback Riding
Sailing
Scuba Diving
Windsurfing

The Neighborhood

Many of us fail to realize that men have to run errands and go about their daily routines in exactly the same places we do. Here's a list of close-to-home places that you may have previously overlooked:

Laundromat
Coffee Shop
Hardware Store (weekends are a prime time; ask someone for advice)
Bicycle Shop
Sporting Goods Store
Home Exercise Shop
Supermarket's deli counter (especially when there's a wait)
Parks on the weekend (divorced dads are out playing with their kids)
Sushi Bar (sit at the counter)

Car or Boat Show
Investment seminars, any class to do with financial matters.

Meeting through Friends

Lots of people like meeting through friends. Couples who
are set up through friends feel more comfortable about meeting
each other since they each come highly recommended. So don't
be shy about letting all your friends—both married and single—
know that you're looking. It may help both of you if you share
your most important non-negotiable needs with your friends. If
you really don't want to date a man with children or if it's
important he doesn't smoke, let that be known.

If a friend does set you up and it doesn't work out, be
gracious about the experience. Thank your friend for her thoughtfulness, and *do not* criticize the man. He may be a close friend
of hers, and you should be sensitive to that relationship. For the
same reasons, be diplomatic about letting him down. Ask her if
there is anyone else she may have in mind for you.

If the date works out, let your friends know you had a good
time, but don't elaborate. Always assume that anything you report
back will be repeated to your date. If you start dating regularly,
it's a good idea to refrain from sharing details of the relationship
with the friend who played matchmaker until you and your
partner are on solid footing. Especially do not comment on his
sexual performance! When you date a friend of a friend, you
have to maintain a little distance for privacy.

Veronica, a 28-year-old nurse, remembers how hard it was
to keep mum about her budding relationship with Gary when
speaking to Laura, their friend in common.

> I wasn't intentionally being evasive whenever Laura
> asked how things were going with Gary, and God knows
> I had lots of questions to ask that she probably had
> the answers to. But I respected her friendship with Gary,
> and didn't think it would be fair to gossip about him
> to someone who knew him well. From the very begin-
> ning, Gary and I discussed the situation and we both
> agreed not to discuss our relationship with her for these

reasons. Even after Gary and I officially became a couple, and it was all right to break the silence, we still were very selective about what information we shared. We let Laura know that this was no indication of how we each felt about her, but was for the benefit of all parties involved. She understood and respected our reasons for doing it.

Blind Date

A few guidelines will help you navigate the tricky waters of a blind date.

First get the facts. Let your friends know that your curiosity must be partially satisfied before you meet him. Get as much information on him as possible, but not too much to ruin the mystery. Find out why they think you're ideal for each other. Presumably they have reasons beyond the fact you're both single and breathing.

Always pre-screen the date. Call him beforehand and plan a mini-date, like coffee or a quick lunch. Never go out with a man just because you feel you owe it to your friends. As always, trust your instincts about a person.

Be in the right mood. Blind dates are like the prizes in Cracker Jack boxes—you never know what you'll get. But that's part of the thrill. If you don't feel enthusiastic about surprises, beg off until a time when you're feeling more adventurous.

Matchmaking

Formal matchmaking has come a long way since *Fiddler on the Roof* types of meddlesome, small-town gossips. Nowadays a matchmaker is more likely to be called a relationship consultant and to have a background in the behavioral sciences along with extensive counseling experience. Matchmaking services operate like all other businesses. Most of their clientele is made up of busy professional career men and women who have little time or opportunity to meet new people.

Most matchmakers depend on extensive personal interviewing techniques to provide them with the information they need to make a perfect match. Though few matchmakers will promise you a specific number of introductions within a year, it is highly probable that the men you do meet will satisfy your non-negotiable needs. Also, the men you do meet through a matchmaker are usually very serious about finding a mate. After all, they, like you, will have made a sizable monetary investment in their love lives.

When a proposed match doesn't "fit," both individuals usually fill out a questionnaire to describe why the match wasn't suitable. The matchmaker pays close attention to this information in order to assess more correctly the kind of match each client requires. If a pattern begins to emerge which seems at odds with the client's stated preferences, the matchmaker will consult with the client to re-evaluate or define more specifically some of her non-negotiable needs.

The quality of services offered by matchmakers varies greatly. As with any professional service, it pays to obtain the names of several matchmaking services in your community and to research each before deciding on any one. Here are questions to ask while interviewing matchmakers or any type of dating service:

How long have they been operating? If you are joining a new service, remember that it usually takes some time for any new business to build up a sizable membership. Also, a new business has no track record to investigate. Bear in mind that the majority of small businesses fail within the first year.

What is the ratio of men to women in the age group you prefer? This is worth knowing. If there are fewer than 40 men to every 60 women in your age group, you can probably do better.

Are the members geographically desirable to you? What good does it do if you live in Los Angeles and all the men who are members live in Alaska? Find out where the majority of male members live and decide whether or not you'd be willing to commute to meet someone.

How long is the membership? Is it possible to freeze your membership? You may not need a lifetime membership in a dating service, but only six months. Don't be pressured into buying something if you only intend to do some dating-service shopping. Freezing your account allows you to become an inactive member if you meet someone and agree to date him exclusively. Then if things don't work out, you become "active" again.

What do other members say about the service? If you don't know anyone who is a member, stop in the restroom or lobby and strike up a conversation with another women who appears to be a member. Ask her opinion. Another good idea is to call the Better Business Bureau or local chamber of commerce to see what they have to say about the company.

Video Dating

Video dating services have grown in popularity. They are set up like clubs, and charge a yearly membership fee. Each candidate is interviewed on videotape. This two- to three-minute tape is then made available for viewing by other members of the club. If you like the tape of a club member, he is notified and given the opportunity to view your video in turn. If he likes your tape as well, the service arranges a way for the two of you to contact each other. All personal information about members is kept in the strictest of confidence.

One benefit of video dating is that you have an opportunity to pre-screen men on the basis of their looks and general demeanor. But unless you're very relaxed and comfortable in front of a video camera, you may not appear to be as friendly and appealing as you are in real life. The same, of course, holds true for the men whose tapes you view. You may want to consider the kind of impression you'll make in front of a camera before joining a video dating club.

Some video dating services offer social events for their members. Since each service differs in price and benefits, it is well worth talking to other members before investing in a particular club.

Singles Dining Clubs

Dining clubs bring together singles who love good food and quality restaurants. Depending on the club, members generally meet at a new restaurant to sample a new cuisine each time out. The procedure at the restaurant depends on the club: some have members change seats with each new course; others have everyone sit next to the same person all evening. If this dating option sounds appealing, find out about the particular club's procedure and its male-female ratio before joining.

Bars

Bars, for better or worse, remain a way for singles to congregate. Despite rumors to the contrary, socializing in bars can be a fun and even productive way of meeting new men. The following suggestions will help you get the most out of the bar scene.

Your luck depends a lot on the mood you're in. If you're not up for the experience, you'll only be wasting your time and money.

Go at the right time. You're better off dropping in casually for Happy Hour at a bar after work to have a snack and a drink. The bar scene on Friday and Saturday nights can be very intense and unless you're up for the meat-market experience, plan other activities for those evenings.

Choose your bar carefully. Bars known as singles bars attract clients who want to pick up women that evening. You want to avoid such bars if you are looking for more than a sexual connection. Also avoid hotel bars filled primarily with married men from out of town. Your best bet is a bar near work where many men stop on their way home.

Many professionals congregate at their own special hangouts—find out the one for your industry. Or, if you have a yen for men in a specific field, say stockbrokers or architects, learn where they go to in your area. Open your conversation by telling the man that you're considering a career change and would appreciate some friendly advice. Look for bars that attract a good mix of men and women, where the feeling is festive as opposed to intense, where you feel comfortable walking in and being by yourself.

Sports bars provide more than simply a way to watch sports events on a large-screen TV. They are always populated with a healthy number of men. If you're a sports fan, a sports bar can be a great setting for you to show off your knowledge of double plays, penalty shots, and forward passes.

Swank restaurants in town often have beautiful bars to match. Find out what the latest hot restaurant is in town, and enjoy the view from the bar.

It may be more comfortable to enter a bar with a girlfriend or two, but men are less likely to approach you than when you are alone. This doesn't mean you should leave your friends at home (sometimes having a friend at their side is the only way women get up the nerve to enter bars!). Simply split up after you arrive. Do, however, plan to touch base with each other throughout the evening.

If you see someone you like in a bar, go up to him. Sometimes the easiest way to get a conversation going is to give the attractive person a warm smile and a friendly hello.

If a man asks for your telephone number, tell him you'll give him your card if he gives you his in return. If you're not sure you want the man to have your number, ask him for his card, and tell him you'll call him.

Nightclubs and Dance Spots

Nightclubs and dance spots are the hands-down favorites among singles. Men and women report they far prefer this form of activity to hanging out at a bar. Clubs provide a common focus—everyone there at least enjoys music, and if a particular entertainer or band is playing, you can find out who else in the crowd is a fan. For those whose feet can't stand still, dancing makes getting to know someone easy and relaxed.

Health Clubs

Since we feel more favorable toward people we meet while enjoying ourselves in comfortable surroundings, a health club is an ideal place to meet men. To make things happen, be open, casual, and friendly to everyone. If you already belong to a club, visit it at different times of the day to see which men show up at which time. Arrange your workout schedule accordingly. Some men attend aerobic classes, but these classes don't offer much opportunity for chatting. A better bet is to position yourself in the weight room and make new friends while firming up. Also, co-ed sauna and steam rooms are other promising locations.

Seminars/Workshops/Classes

Sooner or later most of us head back to the classroom. Whether it's a workshop for on-the-job advancement or courses to obtain necessary credentials, or an adult education class you've always wanted to take, these relaxed settings bring you together with many men who have similar interests.

If you decide to take a seminar or class just in order to meet someone, use your head when you pick your topic. You'll be less likely to meet a man in a course on interior design or stencil painting or quilting and more likely to meet one in a session on computers, finance, real estate, or mechanics. One tried-and-true tip: get to the class early, and stand toward the back of the room to observe classmates entering (don't be obvious about this). When someone who looks interesting sits down, that's your signal to do the same—close to him!

ADVERTISING

Advertising offers one of the most successful modern methods for finding men who will appeal to you. By placing a personals ad you put yourself in the desirable position of choosing rather than being chosen. As you sift through your fan mail, you will decide which men seem interesting enough to consider calling, and even meeting. Men's responses to personals ads outnumber women's by thirty to one. For this reason alone, you should consider the personals an easy, effective way to meet a large pool of men quickly.

Despite the increased popularity of personals ads, many women still express negative feelings about placing an ad. They believe only kinky people looking for sex slaves, or couples in "open marriages," or the desperately lonely place ads. But actually ads are safe, efficient, and get quick results. When I placed my personals ad I was not kinky, sex-starved, or desperate, but I was very busy. A male friend of mine had met the woman he had been dating for months through an ad, so I thought I might give it a try. I knew I couldn't possibly meet men any stranger than the ones I'd already been meeting anyway. This is the ad I placed.

Blonde Belle Seeks Beau

Attractive blonde belle, 26, 5'7", 125 lbs. complete with soft drawl, pale skin, and parasol, seeks the Rhett of her dreams. If you're an attractive, athletic W/M 30–40, 5'11" or taller, financially secure, emotionally stable, and curious enough to answer this ad, I'd like to show you a little Southern hospitality.

Within a week of my ad's publication, I received a big, fat, manila envelope filled with responses from men who wanted to meet me. Just the week before I had been lonely, and now I was getting fan mail!

I was surprised by the quality of men who answered my ad. Many responded because they were busy professionals who didn't have time to meet women or generally hated the singles bar scene. Of course, there were a few married men and some definite weirdos in the batch, but I expected that. It made no difference because the process is 100 percent anonymous.

The letters proved to be an effective way for me to screen men. By knowing in advance about a man's background, I avoided those who I felt "off limits" from the start. It's sometimes easier to acknowledge facts about a man which make him totally unsuitable for you before you meet him. Once you have met a man and become smitten with him, it's usually too late to be objective.

After culling from my 70 respondents the 7 most likely candidates, I pulled out my appointment calendar, called each one of them, and set up meetings at a local restaurant. I met one or two each day for the next five days, usually spending about half an hour over coffee.

My husband, Neal, was among the first. The chemistry between us was electric from the start. But I was determined to meet all seven men on my list and to take my time choosing among them.

After a week of meeting and screening, I finally began dating the three best possibilities, Neal included. Because I had more than one man in my life, I found it easier to maintain my perspective. This was a new experience for me since until then I had dated only one man at a time. I also felt better prepared entering dating situations with these three. Their letters had informed me more about them than many of the men I had dated had ever told me in person. I felt in control of my love life for the first time, and that felt wonderful.

Phyllis, a 37-year-old computer software designer, had recently ended a two-year relationship when she decided to place a personals ad. She wanted to meet a number of men and wanted the ad to be playful, but she also wanted to get the message across that she was looking for a long-term relationship. This is the ad she ran.

Be My Valentine
Luscious, long legged, red-headed lady, 36, 5'7", seeks a man 35-45 willing to be my Valentine every day of the year. If you are attractive, romantic, single, and wish to spoil and be spoiled by an attractive, independent woman, send hearts and candies to:

Phyllis ran the ad for two weeks in three different newspapers and received 52 replies, many with candy and Valentine cards. The sister of one man, Andrew, an engineer whose company had just transferred him to the Bay area, had seen the ad and suggested he respond to it. As his sister knew, Andrew had a weakness for redheads. He sent Phyllis a handmade Valentine with a brief note and his phone number. The two met, hit it off immediately, and within a year they married.

Barbara, a 37-year-old partner in a successful marketing company, tells what led her to the personals.

A few years ago I decided to take a closer look at what I wanted in my life. That's when I went into a business venture with two other partners. During that fast-track time, I was more interested in career development than romance. Then a year ago, I began to yearn to be part of a couple again. Looking back, all of the men I had dated had been outside the mainstream—actors or artists. Now I wanted to date a different kind of man— the kind who was more marriage-minded and stable. Last year I decided that meeting a potential mate would be one of my personal goals for the year. To this end, I also made specific short-term goals. For instance, my goal in September was to have a New Year's date with a man I really liked.

I began reading books on the subject of relationships, and it seemed they all discussed women's emotional problems. I didn't have a problem—I just needed direction. When I attended your workshop, it made absolute sense to me. You advocate the same concepts used every day in business. Your strategy for finding a mate was the same process as mapping out an executive recruiting plan to hire a CEO.

Barbara decided to place the following ad in two local papers.

Tall Sensual Brunette

Comfortable in box seats at Candlestick or the ballet. SWF, well educated, high energy, pretty entrepreneur, age 37, w/offbeat sense of humor, a dazzling smile and very busy schedule has time for you if you're 35 to 45, handsome, ambitious and ready for a one in a million woman. Non-smoker. Photo appreciated. Barbara, PO Box ...

She ran the ad for two weeks and screened down the "applicants" from 80 to 20.

Fifteen of the men I considered to be potential mates, and five others I planned to establish friendly relationships with. After meeting all the men, there were three I was most interested in. One was a sports writer, one, an emergency room physician, and one was a business executive.

After dating for a few months, Barbara realized that the man she liked best was a commitophobic and they had to break up. However, looking back on the experience, Barbara claims she still thinks its a good way to meet men and she would try it again.

Placing an ad forces you to identify the kind of man you are looking for. Lori, a 42-year-old dentist, said she could not have written an ad without first determining her non-negotiable needs. It would have been totally non-productive.

I wouldn't have known what I was looking for. My

non-negotiable needs were that a man be emotionally
mature, verbal and expressive, intellectual, sexy, and
supportive of my goals. I didn't meet my boyfriend
through the ad but as a result of placing it, I became
more aware of what I was looking for and realized a
long-time friend fit the description of my ideal mate. I
took a chance and appealed to him in a different way,
and we are now engaged to be married.

Renda, a 40-year-old physical therapist who was recently
divorced, discovered that placing an ad did more than get her
back into the dating scene quickly and painlessly.

Placing the ad was an incredible boon to my ego. It
made me realize there are more fish in the sea and it
helped me keep perspective. I didn't rush into the first
relationship that came my way after my divorce because
I had a notebook filled with men who wanted to keep
me distracted. I dated many different men and am still
dating. For now I'm just shopping around but eventually
I do want to marry again.

How to Design an Ad

Develop an angle. Focus on your best asset. If you have a
strong sense of humor, show it off by writing a really funny ad.
If you have an interesting career, are an expert in a particular
field, or have unusual hobbies, let that aspect of your life determine
the tone and content of the ad.

Connie, who runs her own successful public relations firm,
used her career as the jumping-off point.

What's Your Angle?

**Attractive, dynamic, brunette, public relations lady, 5'6"
seeks personal relations with articulate, fun loving, financially secure guy for more than just a few press releases.
Send your story and angle to:**

Connie was skeptical at first about placing the ad, but two
weeks later, after receiving over 100 responses, she quickly changed

her outlook. Dennis, the man she eventually married, responded
to her ad with a press release describing his attributes, interests,
and outlook on life. He also included an article that had been
printed in a business magazine about his public relations firm. It
included a photo of him and Connie recognized him as someone
who had spoken at a networking event she had recently attended.

> I had really enjoyed his presentation, found him very
> handsome and wanted to introduce myself, but he was
> surrounded by people afterwards and I just lost my
> nerve. I couldn't believe my luck when he responded
> to my ad. I had a second chance to connect with him
> and I went for it.

Connie called Dennis immediately and set up a coffee date.
After meeting her, he said he remembered her from the networking
event and had planned to introduce himself, but she had disappeared before he'd had a chance to find her. Through her ad
Connie met several other men she thought had romantic potential
and dated them all. After three months both she and Dennis
agreed that they were meant for each other and they agreed to
date exclusively. A year later they were married.

Adrianne also used her job as a springboard for her ad. A
talk show host, Adrianne wanted a relationship that wasn't casual.
She was able to get this point across using a phrase connected
with her profession.

Tantalizing Talk Show Host
**39, 5'2", who looks as good as she sounds seeks articulate,
attractive, emotionally stable man (35–45) for more than
just a guest appearance in my life. Photo optional.**

The ad ran in a Florida singles paper, and pulled an as-
tounding 150 responses in just two weeks. Of them, Adrianne
screened the number to 18, and met all of them all within a
three-week period. She eventually narrowed down the competition
to three and is presently choosing from among them.

The following ad which I designed for Sandra, a 34-
year-old attorney, drew more responses from the *Pacific Sun*
than any other that year. This ad has a great deal of sex
appeal.

Luscious Long Legged Redhead
Green-eyed, slim (5'7"), sophisticated lady who is at home
on land or sea, seeks first class mate for romance, intrigue,
and more. If you are 35–45, handsome, successful, funny,
fit, and daring enough to answer this ad, you may be in
for the adventure of your life.

One man Sandra met said he never expected her to live up
to the fantasy he had of her before they met, but had been
pleasantly surprised. Men felt the ad conveyed that Sandra was
someone special, and they were curious to meet the woman behind
the ad. After Sandra confessed the ad had been designed by a
"romance consultant," all of the men thought it was a great idea,
though they laughed because it sounded so funny. Sharing her
secret was a great way to break the ice.

This is what Sandra had to say about her experience with
the personals:

> Even if I don't meet the man of my dreams, it has been
> the most clarifying experience I've ever had. I've really
> been forced to look at what the most important things
> are for me and sometimes it's not easy to be honest
> with yourself. For instance, I don't like to think I'm the
> kind of person who cares about the way a person looks.
> I thought I would change if I met the right man and
> looks wouldn't matter. Now I realize it really does matter
> to me; it's a non-negotiable. I don't want a man who
> has a slight build or is shorter than I am. I'm just not
> attracted and I'm finally acknowledging that that's the
> way it is.
>
> I also thought money and success was important,
> but I'm meeting so many men in succession that fit that
> role I'm finally recognizing the pattern. They're all too
> interested and involved in their careers to be able to
> give fully in a relationship. Making a ton of money isn't
> enough. Even though I know I'm supposed to know
> already what I'm looking for, I realize that for me, and
> probably many other women, it takes "hands on" ex-
> perience with dating many men. The personals gives

you that opportunity to meet many men, not only through your ad, but as a result of it too. Doesn't it always seem men come around when you're dating a lot? As soon as I placed the ad and started meeting men, the feedback I was getting was so good—and I wasn't thinking about myself that way at the time. It really boosted my confidence. Men from my past started coming out of the woodwork and picking up something different about me. I started meeting men everywhere I went, even at the grocery store.

I was really surprised by the quality and variety of men who responded. I've screened down to ten men so far and am still receiving responses. I think I'll probably date four. I would say the ad was an absolute success and that every women should run an ad at least once to clarify what she really wants. My therapist agrees that even if Mr. Right isn't among the men I meet, it has still been a great learning experience.

Another approach is to use a hobby. Laura, a 32-year-old financial sales representative, used her avid interest in sailing.

Shapely Seafaring Brunette

32, 5'6", seeks handsome, shipshape first mate 30 or over who's in the mood for a leisurely sail into the sunset with the right woman. If you're ready to throw your compass overboard and seek true adventure, I'd like to throw you off course. Reply to:

Make sure the hobby you select really interests you, since it will be the main reason why men will answer your ad.

Marcia, a 32-year-old special events coordinator, had recently broken up with her boyfriend when she came to see me about designing an ad. Marcia had a big advantage with her "sports fan" theme because most men love sports. The image this ad must have conjured up in men's consciousness overwhelmed Marcia with responses.

Shapely Blue-Eyed Blonde

Sports fan, 34, successful and sane, seeks exciting overtime with WM, 35-45, who is financially secure, emotionally

**stable and seeking home base with a sophisticated, sensual
tomboy. Send game plan and photo to:**

The toughest part about placing an ad for Marcia was not
being overwhelmed by all the replies and her temptation to date
men only because they looked handsome in their photos.
Marcia ran her ad in August, one of the slowest months of the
year to run an ad because so many people take vacations then.
Even so, it was popular. Marcia received close to 100 replies from
three different newspapers. One man she met and would like to
start dating, a 41-year-old real estate investor, didn't even see
the ad himself. A friend cut it out of the paper and gave it to
him. He was a real sports fan himself and during their conversation on the phone, they found out they'd even gone to the same
small college back east.

Marcia had the following to say about her experience so far
with the personals.

> I would suggest it to anybody. I used to think, who are
> these people who answer these ads? Before it seemed
> artificial. Now I realize they are people who are busy
> like me, and mostly well educated. My intention is to
> date at least four people.

Marcia also feels it's easy to get sidetracked by paying attention only to how a man looks in his photo. Looks may be
important to you, but don't disqualify a man too soon if he's not
exactly your type. If there are other things about him that indicate
some mutual interests, you should consider meeting for coffee.
Sparks may fly if you meet him in person. As Marcia said,

> Getting photos with a man's response is not always so
> good. Sometimes a photo can do you a disservice because
> if he's too good-looking, he probably just wants to play.
> On the other hand, if he's not great-looking in the pic-
> ture, you may not want to meet him, but he might look
> better in person or have some fine qualities. Because I
> have a weakness for very good-looking men, maybe
> next time I shouldn't ask for a photo. About 75 percent
> of the men who responded sent one.

Use a Bold Headline. A bold, catchy lead-in line will make your ad stand out. Be creative or funny, or use an appealing description of yourself. Don't be shy about using words like "sensual," "sexy," "attractive." Appealing descriptions pull like crazy and the earlier they appear in the ad, the better.

Keep It Short. Don't waste your time and money telling your life story. No one reads an ad that goes on and on. Moreover, a long ad gives the impression that the author is desperate or neurotic. Stick to the basics, and leave something to his imagination.

Include the Essentials. Mention your age, race, marital status (divorced, for instance), a physical description, and a personality description. Also, if you're adamant about issues like not smoking or pets or men with children, you should mention these too. To identify the type of man you're looking for, refer to your list of non-negotiable needs and your description of an ideal mate. If you're looking for a certain age, height, or profession, be sure to mention such matters. If you're interested in meeting men only in a certain age range, you had better be specific. Otherwise your mailbox will be cluttered with responses from men of all ages.

Use an Alias. Men prefer to answer an ad that has a name attached to it. Use a name you like, and then when you call him up, share your secret about using an alias and you'll have established an instant bond. If you place an ad in several newspapers, use different names to help keep track of which paper pulls best in case you run an ad in the future.

Seeing is Believing—or is it? Should you request a photo? If looks are very important to you, you may want to request a photo, but bear in mind the drawbacks. Many good-looking men simply don't possess photos of themselves. Also, by insisting on photos, you may discriminate against perfectly gorgeous men who are, like most of us, camera-shy. Even men with photographs may feel self-conscious about getting recognized by you at some point in the future—whether you contacted them or not. One solution to this dilemma: include "photo optional" or "reply with photo gets automatic response" as the last line of your ad.

Give Your Ad Maximum Exposure

You'll get better results if you run your ad for two or three weeks and in different papers (consider singles publications, city magazines, alternative newspapers, and special-interest publications). Many men who want to respond may forget to or may be too busy the first time they read it. Expect about a week to go by between the time a man notices your ad and when you actually receive his letter.

Keep It Private

Most personals sections have rules on this subject anyway, but just so you know, don't include your address or phone number. Take out a box number offered by the paper so your replies can be forwarded to you safely and efficiently.

Time Your Ad Properly

Place the ad when you can devote one or two weeks to following up on your responses. Otherwise, you will have wasted your time and energy, not to mention money, placing the ad. Experts say the best time of the year to place or answer an ad is in the spring or fall. Next best is winter, and summertime is the least favorite.

The Three Major Mistakes When Writing Personals Ads

Using the dreaded "C" word. The word that strikes terror in the hearts of single men the world over doesn't sound any prettier when it's in black and white. Sure, you're after a commitment, and a long-term one at that, but never come out and say so in an ad. Men don't want to "commit" to an ad. However, they will want to meet a woman who sounds interesting, and that could lead to anything.

Listing predictable interests. It's a rare person who doesn't like taking long walks on the beach, sitting in front of a fireplace, or enjoying lazy Sunday afternoons! The less generic and more specific your ad becomes, the greater the likelihood you'll hear from men who are one-of-a-kind themselves! So take a chance and boldly state what you're about. If you have a "Far Side" sense of humor, won't miss a concert by Bruce Springsteen, and own a Garfield the Cat collection to boot, say so! You'll be surprised at the number of souls out there who share or are attracted to one or more of your interests.

Writing a group ad. Although there is strength in numbers, and many women feel more comfortable designing an ad that invites men to attend a mini dinner party held with other women, this approach to meeting men is fraught with far too many problems to be recommended. First, many men are reluctant to respond to an ad placed by two or more women, unless they themselves have friends to "double" with. Then there is the jealousy factor—what if both men invited to a dinner party for four clearly prefer you, or the one you're interested in likes your friend, and the one she's more attracted to is attracted to you? For friendship's sake, it's best for friends to place ads on their own and compare notes later.

Friends can be a great moral support, however, as you write your ad, screen the answers, and get up the courage to arrange interviews. We all need people to help us put our best self forward and to cheer us on when we do things that are difficult or risky.

Writing a Dynamite Ad, Step-by-Step

GENERAL ADS

The Romance Management worksheet titled How to Advertise for a Mate will give you ideas about words you can use in your ad. Take enough time to relax and get your creative juices flowing. Free associate to come up with a theme for your ad. Think about your hobbies, career, goal in life. Also recall how those close to you have described you.

When I helped Joanne, a 34-year-old real estate broker, write an ad, we first free-associated about her job. The words that came up were real estate, property, a good investment, appreciation, assets, long-term investments.

Describe yourself physically. We settled on Joanne's three most important physical attributes—cute, brunette, 5'7".

Describe your personality. One word summed it up for Joanne—zany.

Describe the type of man you're interested in. Joanne wanted a man who was between 32 and 42, handsome, eligible, stable, and looking for a long-term relationship.

Decide whether you want a general ad which will pull a large number of responses or a specific ad that will pre-screen

HOW TO ADVERTISE FOR A MATE

Personality descriptions

accomplished
active
adorable
adventurous
affectionate
ambitious
ardent
articulate
artistic
attentive
balanced
bold
bright
brilliant
career-oriented
charming
cheerful
communicative
compassionate
complex
conservative
crazy
creative
cultured
curious
cynical
dependable
doesn't take self too seriously
down to earth
distinguished
dynamic
earthy
East Coast vitality
easy-going
easily amused
effervescent
elegant
energetic
enthusiastic
exciting
expressive

extraordinary
extroverted
exuberant
fantastic
fascinating
feminist
flexible
frank and feisty
fully alive
fun-loving
fun to be with
funny
generous
gentle
gracious
gutsy
happy
have integrity
heartful
high-intensity
high visual appetite
homebody tendencies
honest
impish sense of humor
impulsive
independent
inspiring
intelligent
inventive
irresistible
irreverent
inviting
jovial
laid back
liberal
light-hearted
listener
lively
love to laugh
loyal
magnificent

mature
mellow
mischievous
natural
new age
nonconformist
nonjudgmental
not pushy
old-fashioned
one-of-a-kind
open-minded
opinionated
optimistic
outgoing
original
outrageous
patient
persistent
personable
positive outlook
positive thinker
poised
playful
polite
powerful
quiet
rebel
refined
romantic
saucy
scintillating
secure
self-assured
self-aware
self-entertaining
self-integrated
self-reliant
sense of humor
sensible
sensitive
sensual

HOW TO ADVERTISE FOR A MATE

Personality descriptions (cont.) *Height*

Personality descriptions (cont.)

serious
shy
sincere
sixties' attitude
socially adept
soft
sophisticated
spirited
spiritual
spontaneous
stable
stellar
stimulating
streetwise
strong
strong-willed
successful
sultry
supportive
sweet
tender
thoughtful
traditional
understanding
uninhibited
unpredictable
unselfish
urban
versatile
vivacious
vulnerable
warm
well-rounded
wise
witty
wonderful
worldly wise
wry
young-at-heart
zany

Height

medium
petite
small
statuesque
tall
tiny
towering

Weight/Shape

athletic
fit
full-figured
full-hipped
in good shape
in great shape
large
lean
medium build
muscular
nice figure
on the heavy side
physically fit
plump
powerfully built
proportionate
queen-sized
Rubenesque
shapely
slender
slightly overweight
solid
trim
voluptuous
well-built
well-proportioned
wiry

Eyes

amber
bedroom eyes
blue-grey
bright-eyed
cobalt
dark blue
dark eyes
deep brown
green
hazel
ice blue
lapis blue
light blue
rich brown
steel blue

Hair

ash blonde
auburn
bright red
curly
deep red
full
honey blonde
light brown
long
Orphan Annie
platinum
salt-and-pepper
sandy blonde
sandy brown
shiny
short
smooth
steel grey
straight
strawberry blonde
unruly

for you. Joanne wanted a large response, so we set about writing a general ad. We zeroed in on what she was seeking and came up with a clever "hook" on the end to guarantee a strong response.

Devise a catchy headline. Using our real-estate theme, we came up with "A Sound Investment."

The finished ad read:

A Sound Investment
Cute and zany brunette real estate lady, 34, 5'7", and slim, seeks male appreciation. If you are 32–42, available and consider yourself prime property, I'd like to make a long-term investment. Let's get together and compare assets.

This ad is an example of a sexy, though not suggestive, ad that draws a large response. Some women say they would feel embarrassed to place such an ad. But why not write one dynamite ad that pulls in many responses rather than a lukewarm ad that only delivers a few letters? Just because an ad has sex appeal doesn't mean men will expect you to go to bed with them right after your first coffee date. If one should suggest such a possibility, don't be shy about setting him straight.

ADS THAT PRE-SCREEN

A specific ad will do your screening for you. It will bring in fewer responses but more appropriate ones. If you have explicit non-negotiable needs in areas such as religion, political persuasion, or having or liking children, it makes sense to mention them in your ad. Here is an example of an ad that pre-screens.

Pretty Single Parent
I'm a 28-year-old, 5'8", slim, brunette dentist with a lovely 6-year-old daughter seeking a single male (perhaps a dad) who would enjoy the company of an affectionate mom-and-daughter combo who love hiking, biking, double features, and Disney World. I have a reliable babysitter and adorable daughter who is open to the idea of mom finding true love. Pets a plus. No smokers please.

How to Screen the Responses

Receiving fan mail can be overwhelming at first. Out of all of these men vying for your attention, how do you separate the true contenders from the rest? Here are some pointers in the selection process.

Start by reading and grading each letter. Your criteria will vary according to your non-negotiable needs. Of course you won't be able to screen for most of your needs, such as sensitivity or emotional stability, which must be experienced first-hand. But you should get a feel for a man by the tone of his letter. Give the letter an A, B, C, D, or F. If you are unsure of a letter, put a question mark on it after the first reading, and read it a second time after you've gone through the rest.

Notice his grammar and spelling. You should, of course, keep in mind that not everyone made school spelling bee champ. You may want to excuse a few misspellings and dangling participles. His stationery is also revealing. Did he make an effort to present his story on attractive stock, or did he just use the nearest lined pad? Examine his handwriting. Unless you're an expert in graphology, however, don't attempt to read too much into his handwriting. The main point here is to notice how the man presents himself.

Eliminate photocopied responses that don't refer to your ad. They are placed by men who answer hundreds of ads compulsively. Also eliminate men who submit very long letters. Keep your sense of humor about these and other off-beat, kinky, or otherwise unacceptable ads. You're bound to run into a few.

Say no to men from out of town. Of course, only you can judge what is geographically acceptable, but if you're getting mail from men in Nevada, and you live in Minnesota, the man may simply be looking for a good time whenever he visits your area. Don't get sidetracked!

Organize the letters according to grade. Eliminate all C's, D's, and F's. My clients keep the A's and B's in a special notebook so they don't misplace them.

Review the remaining letters. Your screening should leave about 10 percent of the total letters received. Note on each letter anything you found appealing or have questions about.

Respond promptly. Keep in mind that men who respond to your ad may be replying to several others as well. If you like the way a man's letter sounds, call him at once! Depending on how diligently you follow up on your responses, you can complete the first screening phase within two weeks.

Making Initial Contact on the Phone

The phone is not a 100 percent effective screening process. It is essential to meet a man before determining whether he may be appropriate for you. The purpose of the call is to make initial contact and set up an interview to meet him in person. Trust your instincts. If it becomes apparent during the phone conversation that he is not your type, don't set up a date or give him your phone number.

Review your most desirable candidates. Call the ones you like the best—say, all the A's first—before moving on to the B's. On each letter, circle in red those subjects or activities you would feel most comfortable talking about. Keep the letter in front of you during the conversation so you can refer to it if necessary.

Call in the early evening during the week. If you have to call his office, early afternoon is best.

Do not leave a message on his answering machine with your name and phone number. You may decide later that you don't want him to have your number. And in any case, you want to be in control of the conversation. This can only happen if you initiate the call.

Keep calling until you reach him. Introduce yourself as the person whose ad he responded to. Ask him if now is a good time to talk. Put him at ease by asking him about something in his letter.

Spend no more than 10 minutes talking to him on the phone before setting up a coffee date. If you spend too much time getting to know him over the phone, your expectations will be raised, and you'll feel disappointed if you aren't instantly attracted to him the moment you meet.

Trust your instincts. If you pick up signals during your brief telephone conversation that tell you not to go through the trouble of meeting this man, follow your instincts. You're better off eliminating a man early in the screening process. If you go ahead and meet him, and then feel discouraged afterwards, you may give up and not meet the rest of the men who answered your ad.

Schedule a meeting during your lunch break or right after you get off work. Either way, set a specific time—30 minutes is suggested—for the get-together. Your meeting is to determine if there is any attraction. If there isn't, the 30-minute time limit allows you to bow out gracefully. If there is, still leave after making sure he has your number. If he's interested, he'll ask you out. If not, you won't feel as rejected as you would have if you'd spent the entire evening with him. Tell him that you have another appointment afterwards to make you feel more comfortable about sticking to the time limit. You want to avoid overexposure and burn-out while carrying out a personals campaign. Limiting the amount of time you spend with candidates will help you do so.

As we've all experienced, turning a man down is one of the most difficult and upsetting aspects of dating. No matter how many times you do it, it never gets easier. Here are three stock approaches to use when you're screening candidates over the phone.

Honesty is the best policy. "I don't think I'd be interested in meeting you, but thanks for replying to my ad."

The old standbye. "My old boyfriend and I decided to patch things up and try it again. If it doesn't work out, I'll get back to you. Thanks for replying to my ad."

All work and no play. "I'm really busy now but will give you a call back when I have some free time. Thanks for responding to my ad."

The Thirty-Minute "Informational" Interview

PLAY IT SAFE

Many women tell me they know more about the men they meet through the personals—before they've met—than they do about men they've met through other channels. Still, there are some basic guidelines to follow to insure personal safety. These guidelines make sense on any first date, regardless of how you were introduced.

- Never invite him to your place or go to his apartment on the first meeting. Plan to meet in a public place, at a restaurant or café. Choose a café that is bustling with people.

- Meet him at the café rather than having him pick you up. Have your own transportation available, or plan to take a cab home or to your next destination.

- Trust your instincts. If you feel uncomfortable in his company, don't make plans for a second date or give him your number. Even if you like him, and a second date is in the cards, you still might consider arranging the next date along the lines of the first one—meeting at a convenient public place, taking your own transportation, and so forth.

RECOGNITION

When you set up your meeting, let him know what you'll be wearing and get a good description of him if you haven't got a photograph. Ask specifics about what he'll be wearing. When you arrive at your meeting place, walk in confidently and locate him as quickly as possible. Offer him a big smile when you meet and make an effort to put him at ease. Doing this will help put you at your ease as well.

THE CONVERSATION

The key is to keep it light. Engaging in small talk will give you a chance to react to each other to see how much you have in common. The purpose of the first interview is to assess whether or not there is any physical and conversational attraction between you. Talk about your work and hobbies for now. Don't share intimate details of your life and past relationships or expect him to do the same. Later you'll have opportunities to get more profound. Here are a few good conversation starters:

His letter. Whatever attracted you to his letter is a good conversational tool. For instance, if he mentioned he likes travel, you might discuss his favorite trips and recount several of your own.

Hobbies. Discuss what favorite activities you both enjoy in your spare time.

The week's headlines. Anything newsworthy is worth discussing, though you may want to avoid intensely debated issues. Make a point of reading the newspaper or listening to the all-news channel on the radio that morning.

What if he asks why you placed the ad? Avoid offering detailed information. A man will be turned off if he thinks you are on a man hunt. Have fun with your answers, so you leave him with the impression that you placed the ad as an adventure.

Flirtatious: I placed the ad in the hope that someone like you would answer it (said slowly with eye contact).

Flip: Oh, just thought I'd try something wild and crazy.

Suggestive: I guess for the same reason you answered it.

What if he asks how many responses you received?

Flirtatious: Why, are you getting jealous already?

Flip: Plenty.

Suggestive: Well, I haven't spent much time at home counting. (Never admit your ad didn't pull well!)

What if he asks what kind of men have been responding to your ad?

Flirtatious: No one that can compare to you. (You have to say this with a grin on your face and right before you leave in order to get maximum impact).

Flip: All kinds.

Suggestive: The kind who knows a good women when they read about her.

WHEN TO LEAVE

If you feel the interview is turning into an inquisition, don't feel obligated to stay and answer all his questions. Simply get up, say good-bye, and leave. The beauty of the brief interview is that you can call it quits at any point if you're not enjoying a man's company.

If you decide he's not your type, don't lead him on. Say something like, "I don't think we have enough in common, but thanks for getting together."

If you are having a good time, still do not stray from the game plan. Leave after 30 minutes, but make sure he has your number and provide him with encouragement to call you. Say, "I've got to go, but I would really like to see you again."

WHO PAYS FOR COFFEE?

Decide this matter ahead of time. If you feel most comfortable paying for your own coffee, don't awkwardly fumble with your wallet when the time comes. Keep your money handy and casually place it on top of the check when it arrives. If he makes an effort to pay, don't argue with him about it. Regardless of your feelings about the issue, don't create an incident over this one time. Just thank him graciously and leave it at that.

Responding To Ads

The flip side to placing ads, of course, is responding to them. Answering ads puts you at a disadvantage in that it places you in a weakened position: you are the one being chosen as opposed to doing the choosing. Also, you are thrust into competition with countless other women also interested in meeting a particular man. For these reasons I don't wholeheartedly recommend answering ads as a way to meet men. However, since many women first get their feet wet by answering ads, and then move on to place ads themselves, it can be a valuable learning experience. Also, many women have successfully met men by answering ads.

Rachel, a 31-year-old president of her own consulting firm, responded to six ads in a local singles paper. She chose ads that she thought were interesting and well written. The following ad is the one Rachel responded to.

A Menagerie
Tall, brown-eyed, handsome man, 35. Quiet as a cat, loyal like a spaniel, fit as an antelope, successful like a lion, and crazy like a fox. Looking for capable female zookeeper for loving and full relationship.

Rachel answered by picking up on the animal theme in the ad:

Woof—or should I start this out with a roar?

Stats—31, 5'6", fiery brown-eyed brunette of Italian descent, with a quick smile. Athletic.

Brief history—Raised in Pennsylvania, educated here and abroad, came West with a presidential campaign, and never went back. When my politicking days were through, I made the natural transition to government consulting, and since then, started my own business.

Personality—I walk up escalators, grow impatient waiting for fast food, yet have long term friendships and a steel-trap memory—and hate to put too much in writing unless I'm getting paid for it.

Want to know more? Please call me after 5:00 p.m. at—.

Leave a message and I'll call you back!

P.S. I'm fond of animals.

TIPS FOR ANSWERING PERSONAL ADS

Choose an ad you find interesting, appealing, and easy to respond to. If there isn't anything in an ad that "speaks" to you, it will be difficult to respond creatively. Scan for ads from people who have interests similar to your own.

Know your terms. Personals have a language of their own. Abbreviations for marital status, sex, and partner of preference are usually easy to understand. But there may be more "subtle" phrases that at first reading may elude even the most savvy reader. Avoid ads that contain the following (unless, of course, the particular behavior interests you): submissive, discreet playmate, no strings attached relationship, uninhibited, afternoon delight, loving but firm, high heels and leather.

Keep the tone upbeat, short, and to the point. Long, involved letters to perfect strangers make you look desperate. Try to keep your reply to one side of one page. Keep it positive—you won't score points admitting you're depressed, hate your job, and are tired of being single. Instead, let your reader know you're happy with your life, friends, interests.

Respond as soon as possible. If his ad is appealing, you're not the only woman who will answer.

Answer more than one ad at a time. That way, you'll increase the chances of meeting more men. Also, it's a form of emotional insurance—the more ads you answer, the greater the possibility that someone call you.

Differentiate each letter you write. When responding to several ads at once, think of giving a special twist to each letter to help you remember which ads you answered when you get calls back. An easy way to do this is to sign each letter with a different alias. Use your middle name, nickname, or sign off with just your initials.

Write rather than type. Handwriting is more personal. An attractive note card always makes a good impression on its recipient. But avoid any card that is suggestive or offers a sentimental message about "feelings" on its cover. Even if you use plain stationery, consider placing it in a brightly colored envelope to help it stand out.

Be discreet. Don't answer personals on your letterhead—you could be writing to someone who knows you. For the same reason, sign your note with only your first name or an alias.

Decide which telephone number to give out. Most letters ask for a phone call from the person who placed the ad. Naturally, if you prefer a written response and feel comfortable giving out an address, ask for a letter. Whether you give him your home or office number, mention specific times when he can catch you. This way you won't be caught off balance by his call. Include in your letter a line like: "I'm in and out of the office all morning, so the best time to reach me is between 2:00 and 3:00 in the afternoon."

Keep copies of each letter you sent out. Paste the ad to the top of your response letter. Write in bright letters the alias you used to respond to the ad. Keep the copy handy near the telephone so you'll be prepared when he calls. If you expect him to call you at the office, leave copies of the letter there as well. If you feel unprepared when he calls—wherever you may be—take down his number and return the call after you've rebriefed yourself.

Keep your phone conversations short. When he calls, stay on the phone no longer than ten minutes. Even though he initiated the call, there's no reason why you can't be the one to suggest meeting for coffee if you like what you hear.

PICTURE PERFECT

Who knows how many ad writers have missed meeting Miss Right because their ads contained those two words that strike horror in everyone's heart: "Photos Appreciated." Of course, it seems like an entirely different matter to request a photo than it is to send one. When you're on the sending end, the request for a photo sounds as if you're going to be judged strictly on your looks. No one likes to feel as if they are entering a beauty competition. And most of us feel uncomfortable sending out photographs to perfect strangers. Nevertheless, you can increase the likelihood of getting a response by sending a photo.

When Neal responded to my ad, he sent a photo and requested one of me before we met. I had a color contact sheet handy and cut off a few frames to him. Proof sheets are relatively inexpensive, and many women feel comfortable using them, since it would be relatively hard for a stranger to recognize you on the street based on these small photos.

If you do intend to send a regular-sized photo, have a friend shoot a roll of color film outdoors in late afternoon or early morning light (times when the light is softest). Don't rummage through your photo collection and send one from three years back, when you were 15 pounds lighter and were a blonde for the summer. If you meet him, which is the desired intent, he'll undoubtedly notice the discrepancy. Also, don't do anything silly like sending a photo with a former boyfriend's head cut out of it. If you are going to send a picture, send a flattering one, or don't send one at all. Send only photos you don't need back. And remember, a little creativity can go a long way, especially for the camera-shy.

Martha, a 28-year-old aerobics instructor, responded to an ad that requested a photograph.

Although I had requested photos from men when I had placed ads, I never realized before how vulnerable it can make you feel. What if he didn't respond after seeing the photo? I would feel really rejected. When I saw Greg's ad, I felt we had so much in common I didn't want the photo to stand in the way. So I sent a baby picture of myself with a brief note saying I had gained a little weight since then, but I still had the dimples. He appreciated the humor, and we got together for coffee. That was over two years ago, and we have been dating ever since.

Dottie, a 34-year-old lawyer, also was hesitant about sending a photo, but for professional reasons.

The man whose ad I was responding to was also a lawyer, and I could very well have known him. It wouldn't have been right to put myself in such a vulnerable position. So I sent him a Picasso postcard with a note saying, "I too am a rare and valuable piece of art. If you want a viewing, we could set up a date." I think that really aroused his curiosity, because he called right away.

HOW TO WRITE A REPLY THAT WILL TRIGGER A RESPONSE

To move your letter to the top of his "A" list, write a response so unique and appealing, it'll make him want to read it over and over. Although your first impulse might be to write, "I'm Jane and I liked your ad. I believe we have a lot in common"—DON'T. Avoid being a carbon copy of the others.

Start by reading the ad closely and highlight the parts that intrigued you. Catch his attention by referring to him in an unusual way—either by the headline he chose or how he described himself in the ad: "Dear Incurable Romantic" or "Dear Reluctant Yuppie" or "Dear Fun-Loving Sailor." If he's a transplant from Hawaii, drop the "Dear" and substitute a warm "Aloha" instead.

Of course, you want to get the point across that you share many of the same interests. Don't simply state this; show it in a dramatic, attention-getting way. Let's say both of you love baseball. Rather than state the obvious, take a different approach: "You and I have probably spent many an evening at Wrigley Field together cheering the Cubs on to victory. From my vantage point over home plate, I bet I've spotted you ordering one Polish sausage too many (are you the one who always orders extra mustard?)"

Take a few risks—the more original and appealing your response, the sooner it will get shifted out of his marginal "B" pile into his "A" pile.

SPEAKING UP

The most difficult part of the personal ads process is handling the phone call—it causes anxiety for both parties. To help get you in the right frame of mind (whether you're the initiator or not), here's a sample script. It is based on the Menagerie ad that Rachel responded to earlier in this chapter. Harry, who placed the ad, is now calling Rachel.

Rachel: Hello.

Harry: Hello, this is Harry. You answered my ad in the *Pacific Sun.* I'm the animal lover. Is this a good time to talk?

Rachel: Yes it is. I just got in from work. I really loved your ad. Do you have pets—you sound as if you do.

Harry: Yes, I have a golden retriever and a cocker spaniel.

Rachel: Oh, I love dogs, I grew up with a cocker spaniel.

Harry: Do you have a dog now?

Rachel: Yes, a black female German Shepherd that I adopted from the SPCA. Her name is Leo.

Harry: Do you live near a park where you walk her?

Rachel: Yes, as a matter of fact I live close to Golden Gate Park. Where do you live?

Harry: Pacific Heights.

Rachel: I know a great coffee shop in your neighborhood called Sweet Delights. Do you ever go there?

Harry: Yes, I love the lemon pound cake they have.

Rachel: So would you like to continue this conversation in person—perhaps get together for a cup of coffee there

sometime this week? My schedule is really hectic this
week, but it would be nice to meet you.

Harry: That sounds fine by me. Any day in particular?

Rachel: What about Tuesday at 2:00?

Harry: Sounds good. How will I recognize you?

Rachel: I'll be wearing a navy silk dress, and carrying a
burgundy brief case. How will I recognize you?

Harry: I've got blonde hair, am 6'2", and will be wearing grey
slacks and a red windbreaker. I'll get there a little early
and try to grab a seat by the door.

Rachel: Well, then I'll see you Tuesday at 2:00.

Harry: See you then, bye.

Rachel: Bye.

TRY, TRY AGAIN

Most women don't realize that placing a personals ad does
not have to be a one-time-only action. You wouldn't refuse to
attend any more parties if you failed to meet someone at the
very first one you were ever invited to. So there's no need for
a "once is enough" attitude when it comes to personals ads.

If anything, it may take two or three ads before you become
an expert at the process. Consider each ad to be an experiment.
If you weren't satisfied with the type of man you were attracting
by describing yourself in one way, try another description. It may
take several attempts before you come up with a winning formula
and meet the type of man you consider to have partner potential.

Laura, whose ad appears earlier in this chapter (Shapely
Seafaring Brunette), didn't get the results she could have from
her ad because of how she handled the response and screening
process. She lost interest in following up on some of the letters,
because she preferred to date one of the first candidates exclusively. When things didn't work out with him, Laura decided to
follow up on some of the other men who answered her ad. Some
of these men were insulted that she had waited so long to respond,
others in the meantime had become involved in relationships.

Don't make the mistake Laura did. If you're going to go to the trouble and expense of designing and placing an ad, follow through and do what it takes to complete the process! Otherwise you'll be wasting your time.

But What if People Should Find Out?

Let's say it works out and you meet the man you marry. How do you tell people how you met? Don't feel as if you have to make up an excuse! There is nothing wrong with meeting someone through the personals ads—the important thing is that you met each other. Consider this—is it socially more acceptable to announce that you met the love of your life in a bar at 2:00 in the morning?

MAKING PROSPECTING A WAY OF LIFE

Women who have been most successful in finding appropriate men to date combine prospecting with other aspects of their lives—such as professional networking, religious activities, athletic pursuits, and vacationing.

Aileen, a 42-year-old vice president of a corporate planning operation, employed a time management consultant to investigate ways she could combine her professional networking efforts with opportunities to meet eligible men. The consultant provided Aileen with the monthly schedules of four business groups whose members were primarily single, male, professional, and in her age group. In addition to making some good business contacts, Aileen met Greg and they worked together professionally before beginning to date. In this way Aileen had a chance to see Greg as a man who was ethical, successful, and dedicated to his work. They are now engaged to be married.

Review your Plan of Action worksheet. Consider what obstacles you must overcome in order to find eligible men to date. Devise a plan to tackle the problem of meeting appropriate men. Ask yourself if you've been using lack of time as an excuse. Examine how you've been spending your free time. Are these activities conducive to increasing your exposure to the kind of men you want to meet? If not, you may want to make a few changes in your lifestyle.

FLIRTING FUNDAMENTALS

Finding the right lifemate is serious business, but you need to take a light-hearted approach. If you've never had trouble attracting men, you may be a natural flirt. If not, you may need a few pointers. There are classes, books, and even videos available to coach you in the subtle art of flirting. An excellent guide which I recommend in my workshop is *The Fine Art of Flirting* by Joyce Jillson, which gives you the low-down on all you need to know about flirting in any situation. Flirting never goes out of style. It can ease you out of the most awkward situations and put you in contact with the most interesting men. With a little practice and patience you can master this valuable skill.

You need to approach flirting without "serious intent." Don't invest too much in the outcome of the experience. Do it the same way you might buy a lottery ticket or place your name in a raffle for a free trip to Hawaii. If something comes of it, great! If not, you won't be devastated. Flirting allows you to try out different facets of your personality and see how men react to them. Find out what works and what doesn't. For example, you may not feel comfortable walking up and introducing yourself to a man but are good at including yourself in conversations that other people are having. Fine. You wait until he is speaking to others and then you mosey over. Some women swear by props for conversational starters. For example, Stephanie, a 38-year-old clothing designer, carries a purse that looks like a telephone. Men and women are so curious about what she's carrying they often strike up a conversation with her. Joanne, a 33-year-old country singer, wears a watch that tells Eastern, Pacific and Central time. When people ask her the time she offers all three.

Other women find props too stagy. Develop your own style of flirting and stick to what works for you. Remember, whatever your style, to get the best results, you should combine your approach with the Romance Management principal of an IPR (Intermittent Positive Reinforcement) schedule (which you are familiar with from chapter 2). The following is a successful flirting scenario incorporating an IPR schedule, positioning, positive re-inforcement conversational starters, and other Romance Management strategies you are already familiar with.

Basic Course in Flirting

What is the good of being in the right place at the right time, if you don't know how to take advantage of the situation? For the uninitiated or simply nervous, here are a few tips on the art of flirting, 1990s style. You don't have to be a *femme fatale* to master the technique, but just be willing to take a few risks.

You are at a party full of single, eligible, gorgeous men. You spot someone appealing across the room.

Eye Contact. Start by trying to make eye contact. What happens when your eyes meet? Does he look quickly away? Calmly direct your gaze at him and judge his reaction. Does he appear to be flattered that you have noticed him? Don't stare but allow yourself to gaze a few seconds longer than usual. He may respond by returning your gaze. If so, you should smile slightly and encourage his interest. Or, he may return your gaze but look away quickly or pretend to ignore you altogether. In this case you can interpret his behavior as flattered that you are interested but shy and unsure of what to do next.

Positioning. Next, assess his interest in you. Don't look his way as much as before, but keep your body language open and appealing as you slowly work your way close to where he is in the room. Once you are in proximity to him, resume eye contact and register his reactions. Some women even position themselves directly in front of or beside a man and "accidentally" knock his drink over or bump into him. Go this far only if you're gutsy, and he's standing by himself.

If he is engaged in conversation, try to enter it. If he is alone, it's up to you to get the conversation rolling. Talk about anything that would be appropriate to the situation. Questions are always good, but remember to ask an open-ended question rather than one he can answer with a yes or no. Instead of asking if he's enjoying the party, ask him if he's known the host very long and how they met. This way you start to establish something in common with him.

Touch. If he is returning your gaze, seems interested, and your conversation is going well, you may want to introduce touch. You can touch his upper arm, shoulders, jacket lapel, hands. Remember, the longer your hand rests on him, the stronger the message that you're interested in him. For the most powerful combination, lean toward a man, touch him while smiling and look into his eyes. He will *know* you are interested.

Here are some examples of flirting techniques in action.

Flirting Scenerio #1

The scene: A conference for independent investors on the subject of how to invest in the stockmarket. Kelly, a 36-year-old marketing executive, is attending. There are at least 100 people registered for the seminar, mostly men.

Positioning: Kelly arrives in plenty of time and sips her coffee while waiting for others to register. Once she spots a man she wants to meet, she seats herself two rows ahead of him to the right, directly in his line of vision. She is friendly and speaks with several men and women around her. Through this indirect approach, Kelly is allowing him to admire her from afar while letting him know she is approachable by appearing open and friendly to others.

Eye Contact: Kelly needs to let him know that she notices him and finds him attractive. Before the seminar begins, she visits the restroom. As she passes him she casually gives him a friendly smile. On her way back however, she doesn't overdo it by looking his way again. She calmly makes her way back to her seat and begins balancing her checkbook. (IPR flirting schedule: appearing interested and then distracted.)

The props: Kelly is carrying the annual report of an obscure company she has been following. She has done her homework and has her own reasons for believing this stock could be a big performer. Also, her notepad has the name of her firm on the outside of it (conversation starters).

The opportunity: At the break Kelly was in no rush to leave her seat. It was his turn to make a move and she knew he'd be more likely to approach her if she appeared to be alone and unhurried. She didn't want to be fumbling with her coat and notebook so she left them behind and slowly moved out of her seat into the aisle. Kelly walked down the aisle confidently meeting his gaze and smiling. He stopped her by saying, "Excuse me, do you work for XYZ marketing? I noticed your notebook. Kelly replied teasingly "Yes I do, but I'm supposed to be home sick so I hope you won't tell anyone" (breaking the ice through humor and a personal disclosure). They introduced themselves. When Kelly asked Doug how familiar he was with the company (stressing similarities), he explained that his company had used their services in the past and he named several people in her office whom she knew. This led to a brief discussion about his work in management with a large mail-order company and his personal reasons for taking the course—to consider a career change (offering a personal disclosure). About 10 minutes into the lively conversation, Kelly remembered she needed to introduce IPR, with a little distancing. She quickly excused herself by saying she had to make an important phone call and then added, "If the seminar begins before I get back, take notes for me!" (creating a reason to make contact again and offering positive reinforcement). Before running off she touched him on the sleeve and said, "I want to finish this conversation" (adding more encouragement and impact to her words through the power of touch). With only five minutes left in the break, Kelly checked in with her office and then returned to her seat a few minutes after the seminar began. At the conclusion of the seminar, Doug and Kelly spoke together another fifteen minutes. Kelly refused his offer for dinner, saying she had other plans but that she would love to see him again (sweet and sour technique). He walked her to her car and she gave him her business card with her home phone written on the back and asked for his. As soon as she got home she made a note on the back of his card to remind her of who he was so that months later, when she was creating a party list, she might send him an invitation if she hadn't already heard from him (sending him a trigger) or might introduce him to one of her girlfriends.

The best approach to take when flirting is to avoid being overwhelmed by any particular man. Instead, take each new encounter into stride, hoping for the best but not necessarily expecting to hear from every man you flirt with. To move beyond simply making eye contact, smiling, and hoping for the best, make comments or ask questions. Convey the message that you are pleasant and open to conversation. It may not lead to anything, but it's worth practicing. Why miss out on some great opportunities to connect with men that you wouldn't ordinarily have?

Flirting Scenerio #2

Natalie, a 34-year-old bookkeeper, could meet men any-where. Her friends all envied Natalie. They said her ability to attract men was phenomenal. When Natalie introduced herself at my workshop, she wasn't anything like I imagined she would be. She didn't look like a movie star or a first-class athlete. She was more cute than glamorous. She told us she had met a man that very evening, on the way over. Standing in a crowded cable car, she just turned to a man and said, "Hold on tight!" Two seats opened up, they took them and began talking. They ended up exchanging numbers and planning to get together later in the week for a drink. Natalie said she's dated several men she met this way, even using the same line! It's not important what you say so long as you say something to get his attention. It can be something mundane, about the weather or asking for the time. Natalie's hidden weapon was her personality. She was open to meeting people in general, not just men.

PURPOSEFUL MEETINGS

If you can conveniently arrange your social life in such a way that you can run into a certain man again and again, the positive impressions will build upon themselves and lead him to admire you more than someone he just met in passing. By seeing you over and over again, a man will begin to feel comfortable enough to ask you out and know that you will accept.

Diana, a 36-year-old, attractive stockbroker, placed herself in the field of vision of a man she had been admiring for months at the health club.

After I'd seen him on the stationery bike a few times as I was leaving the Club, I began showing up a half hour earlier. I positioned myself two bikes down from him, and we nodded at each other. One day I brought a copy of *Sports Illustrated*, and he made a comment about an article I was reading. That night he asked if I wanted to go out to grab a bite to eat. We've been working out together and dating ever since.

With a little ingenuity you can invent ways to meet on purpose as naturally as you brush your teeth. Jean, a 32-year-old bookkeeper, was at the veterinarian with her dog Pepper when a gorgeous man with a puppy came in and sat beside her. He told her how his dog of 15 years had died only a week before and that he had just found this stray puppy. The dogs provided them with plenty of conversational material, but Jean knew she had to think fast before this man disappeared from her life forever. She told him she understood how difficult it was to get over the loss of a pet. Adopting the puppy was a good first step, she told him, but he might also enjoy socializing, and it just so happened that she was holding a party at her place the following week. He accepted the invitation and Jean gave him her address. She then went home and started inviting friends over to the party she instantly created. He came to the party, spoke to her at a greater length there, and the two have been dating for six months now.

Instead of asking a man out, you can extend a subtle invitation for him to join you at some activity. Weave enough information into the conversation about the specific time and place where you will be, and, in all likelihood, he'll show up if he's interested. Margie, a 36-year-old home-health-care professional, was interested in Martin, a florist in her neighborhood. They'd engage in small talk when she came in to pick up flowers, but he never asked her out. Margie figured Martin was shy and decided to offer him a little encouragement. One afternoon, when she knew business would be slow, Margie brought in a flyer about an art exhibition that featured a friend's piece of art. After they chatted for a while about the show, she invited him to drop by the gallery that evening, saying "I hope to see you there!" She then gave him a big smile and left. Though Martin knew nothing about art, he showed up at the gallery and spent the evening talking to Margie. The next time they met, he asked her out, and they've been appreciating art—and each other—ever since.

RELAXED SETTINGS

The situations in which you meet men will also make a difference in your ability to strike up conversations and your overall openness. Your "comfort level" is what is critical here. Many women favor relaxed settings, where you are more likely to be yourself and feel less pressured to make a good impression. Some relaxed settings include health clubs, special interest groups, organizations and classes, and the homes of friends.

Debra, a 38-year-old insurance sales representative, discussed how being in a relaxed setting helped her feel and act more approachable.

I tried meeting men at bars or clubs, but I always felt uncomfortable in those settings since the only reason I was going was to meet someone. I know I didn't look approachable because I didn't feel that way. Finally, I got invited to a party a friend gave. That evening I met and ended up dating two men. Also, a woman at the party later introduced me to her old boyfriend and we went out. I feel much more relaxed in someone's home even though I may not know many people there. For me, bars are too competitive and impersonal.

Donna, a 48-year-old engineer, has always enjoyed hiking. With encouragement from a friend, she joined the Sierra Club.

I met many new friends through the Club and found the hikes and day trips enjoyable. I found it easy to open up under those circumstances, and, without even trying, soon fell into a friendship with Dave, a pediatrician whom I met on one of the hikes. We were friends for about four months before we began dating. Hiking together in a group gave us a chance to get to know each other slowly without feeling pressured.

Alexandria a 38-year-old winery executive met her husband in a coffee shop. She was 36 at the time, and he was 42, and neither of them had been married before.

I was in a coffee shop when I spotted a man across

the room whom I found very attractive. The smile he
sent to me was so kind and open. I consider myself
modest, but I knew I'd have to make contact with him
or he'd walk out of my life forever. He left the restaurant,
walked towards his car, but rather than getting in and
driving off, he threw his briefcase in and then took off
down the street. I guessed he had gone to run an errand.
I took out my business card, wrote on the back of it,
"brunette at coffee shop," and walked over to his antique
Mercedes convertible to put it on his windshield. Suddenly he walked up to me out of nowhere and said
hello. I said to him, "I want you to know I don't
ordinarily do this, but I think you look like the kind of
man who would appreciate a good glass of wine." I
then handed him my business card with the name of
the winery I worked for and said I'd like to share a
bottle of Chardonnay with him sometime. He said he'd
like that, introduced himself, and asked if I couldn't
spend the day with him! I let him know I had to get
to work, and left after we talked a little more. He called
me later that day and we've been inseparable since. We
dated about a year and a half before we married.

TRIGGERS

Assume you just met a man. You let him know you were
interested in him, he has your number, and you're hoping he
will call. You need to trigger his memory of you in those cases
when you planned to get together but nothing was ever firmed
up. Although the techniques differ slightly, triggering his memory
is as effective on your fortieth anniversary as it is to procure your
first date.

- Always make a mental note of the topics you covered in
  conversations with men you meet. As soon as you can,
  jot down the details in a dating diary, which also gives
  the date and circumstances of your meeting.

- If you haven't heard from a man in two weeks after
  meeting him, send a newspaper clipping, a cartoon, a

quote, a postcard, or a magazine article which was relevant to your conversation. This will trigger his memory of you and your discussion. If he had been busy, and wanted to call, he may have felt awkward about having waited so long. Your trigger lets him know you remember him fondly, and it presents him with an automatic topic of conversation to use when he calls. You have paved the way for him to make contact with you.

- If after sending a trigger, you don't receive a response within a reasonable amount of time, put that man out of your mind. Send out triggers to other men who also interest you. This technique allows you to increase the possibility of dating men you prefer without actively pursuing them. If you send a trigger and nothing comes of it, you won't feel embarrassed or rejected, since it was only a friendly gesture. On the other hand, if the trigger has its desired effect, a man who initially was not interested may reconsider you as a result of your thoughtfulness. The man who was interested, but got distracted, will be jolted into action to pick up the phone to call.

Here are popular triggers to use.

- A funny cartoon.

Diane, an attractive 34-year-old industrial psychologist, used trigger to attract the attention of an attractive author.

At a book-signing event I attended, the author turned out to be very attractive and single. Rather than audition for a date as several women were already doing, I decided to flirt and send a trigger later. Before meeting him, I grabbed one of his books and skimmed the jacket. It was a murder mystery. Since I hadn't read it, I complimented him on the jacket cover and asked him if he helped design it. We chatted briefly for a few minutes; I bought the book and left. Since he didn't have my number and had met so many people that day that he may have forgotten my name, I made sure he remembered me when I sent my trigger.

The trigger I sent was a list of bestselling fiction books. The note accompanying it said, "You can't judge a book by its cover, but after reading yours, I wouldn't be surprised to see it soon reach the top of this list." I signed my name and also included my telephone number. The trigger not only got me a call from him a few days later, but also a two-year relationship.

Diane realized she had been using this technique for years with her clients. "It's personalized and takes the individual client's interests into account." She now keeps a separate file for men that she wants to trigger.

When the right trigger comes along, I send it out with a brief comment and a business card. Sometimes I even send separate copies of the same trigger to different men, but I always make a note of who got what and keep it close to my phone. That way, when a man calls, we're on the same wavelength.

• A postcard of his favorite vacation spot.

Ellen, an outgoing, 36-year-old dentist, and Andrew, a musician, met at a party but had an opportunity to speak only briefly since he was performing all night and took just one break. Ellen didn't want to hang around late like a groupie and Andrew didn't feel comfortable about pursuing a guest. Luckily, Ellen sent a trigger. During their brief chat, Andrew had mentioned he was looking forward to a video he was doing in Hawaii, his favorite vacation spot, that summer. Ellen picked up a campy postcard of Hawaiian dancers and palm trees and wrote, "I really enjoyed listening to you sing Saturday night, especially the slow songs. Good luck with your video. Aloha, Ellen." He responded shortly after receiving her card and they began dating.

• An article about something you discussed.

When Annie met Allen at a conference, she began a conversation about airfare expenses and how difficult it was to find a good deal. A few days later she saw an article in the paper about discount rates, cut it out, and sent it to him with a note and her card, saying, "I guess there is hope after all!" Allen had already seen the article but used it as an excuse to phone Annie anyway and they decided to get together and begin dating.

PLAYING THE NUMBERS GAME

If you were unemployed, and interviewed for a job at a company where you really wanted to work, would you simply stop the job search after that interview and sit at home waiting until you heard from that one employer? No, in all likelihood, you would continue to interview, exploring options with other companies, perhaps hoping to find an even better opportunity. Approach your love life as intelligently as you approach your job opportunities. Keep your options open. Finding a partner boils down to a numbers game.Since you might have to meet one or two hundred men before finding one sufficiently compatible to be your mate, it's best to put yourself in contact with as many men as possible. If you date several men, you have the opportunity to increase your social skills. You'll feel more desirable, be less likely to over-romanticize your relationships, and more likely to remain objective. Best of all, the larger field of candidates will increase your chances of meeting the right man sooner rather than later.

Use this checklist to see whether you've begun prospecting.

- I know what my non-negotiable needs are.

- I have filled out my plan of action sheet and chosen five places to prospect.

- I know how to be approachable and flirt.

- I dress in a way that enchances my figure and attracts attention.

- I participate in activities that increase my self-esteem while seeking a mate.

- I am prepared with a few short stories that highlight my interests and outlook on life so that when I meet someone

I will present the lively and interesting person I am and rather than feeling tongue-tied because I've been caught off guard.

ROMANCE MANAGEMENT RULE #3:

You need to give yourself permission to have the type of relationship you deserve, a good one.

ROMANCE MANAGEMENT RULE #4:

Be in the right place at the right time, pursuing thought-out goals—on purpose.

DATING SMART

I'm rough, ambitious, and I know exactly what I want. If that makes me a bitch, okay.

—MADONNA

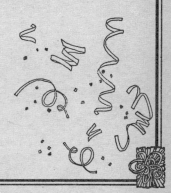

UNLESS you're anticipating an arranged marriage, dating is the only way you can get from meeting to marriage or a long-term relationship with a man. This chapter is all about taking the pain out of dating so you can relax and enjoy the process. One shortcut in the process is keeping a dating diary. If you've ever kept a diary, you know how helpful it is to look back with some perspective on your past and gather valuable insights for your future. For that reason I suggest you keep a dating diary to write down all the valuable information that can help you decide whether or not a particular man has romantic potential. Included in your dating diary will be the answers you provide for the Romance Management worksheets in this chapter as well as your non-negotiable checklist (which you also keep pinned to your bra or anyplace else where it's too uncomfortable to forget about). This chapter will prevent you from being swept away by the wrong men and will help you clearly recognize the right men.

As we all know, the first few dates can be stressful, but with the right strategy, you can make them fun and register a positive, lasting impression on a man in the process.

It's ideal if the man spontaneously asks you out on your first date. If not, you must trigger his memory in order to give him a second chance to call you. If he doesn't respond, you can either forget him or do the asking yourself. Either way, don't feel guilty about dating more than one man at a time. It'll give you twice the chance of meeting the right man in half the time.

THE BUILDING BLOCK APPROACH TO DATING

Mini Dates

A mini date is a shorter version of the standard date. The following schedule offers you a way to build up the amount of time you spend with a man slowly.

A coffee date. This is the least investment in time and energy you can make to meet a potential mate. Don't feel guilty about not spending an entire evening with a total stranger. A coffee date is the most time-efficient and practical approach to take. Once you get the hang of it, you'll swear off regular dates with men you hardly know.

Lunch during the week. Lunches are less time-consuming and less formal than dinner dates. You get a closer look at him without having to spend a whole evening.

Brunch on the weekend. Brunch lets you take time to digest your impressions of him. If you like him and the feeling is mutual, your next step is an activity or a dinner date.

An activity. Athletic pursuits such as bike riding, walking, and sailing are good date activities. When doing physical things, men are more relaxed and can express themselves more emotionally. Moreover, the activity means that you've already shared pleasurable experiences. Dinner is not an ideal first date. Dinner conversations can resemble interrogations during the first few dates. By doing something athletic, you remove the pressure to discuss your lives.

A visit to a museum, auto show, street fair, amusement park. All these activities take the focus off the two of you and place it on something else. You no longer focus on the outcome of the relationship because you are already gaining something from it. As with physical activity, doing things together helps you develop a history together. You share common interests.

Don't leave long unplanned blocks of time on the date. If there are no structured activities, the man thinks he must press for sex. Avoid the problem by keeping him busy.

The First Date

As in any other area of your life, it helps to be prepared before you go out on a date. You want be in the proper frame of mind so you can enjoy the evening rather than being worried about minor details. First of all, you may not be feeling as confident as you normally do because you may be worried about making a good impression. This is where your attitude is so important.

Remember that you are not on a mission to make a man

fall in love with you. Instead, you are interviewing men for the lucky position of your long-term lover or even life mate. There is a big difference. It is important to make a good impression but remember to hold a little in reserve. You don't want to overwhelm a man by telling him all the wonderful things about you too soon. You may sound too eager to impress him or, if he's a little insecure, he might feel intimidated. It's more intriguing to let your life slowly unfold than to offer your life history all in one night. What would you talk about on the second date?

You may not feel as confident as you would like when you're about to go out on your first date with a new man, but there are certain steps you can take to put yourself at ease and project a more positive image. You need to take the time to be prepared for the evening in order to enjoy it fully.

The following specific actions will help to make you confident and relaxed from the start.

Stick to an outfit that you've worn before. If possible it should be one you've received compliments on, one that makes you feel attractive and comfortable. Don't wear a new or unusual outfit that may make you feel self-conscious.

Don't spend too much time getting ready. Spending lots of time in preparation only raises your anxiety level. Choose what you'll wear ahead of time and don't start experimenting with your hair or make-up. If you overdo it, you'll look like you're trying too hard.

Prepare something to look forward to after the date. The treat you choose will keep your spirits up and give you necessary perspective on the evening. Some rewards for after a date include: an interesting show taped on the VCR, a movie rental, a new book, a luxurious bubble bath, or brunch the next morning with a good friend. It's ideal to reward yourself immediately upon arriving home, but the following day can be just as effective if you're not a night owl.

Allow yourself a few minutes to relax before he arrives. Choose a comfortable spot and visualize a time when you were feeling very confident and sure of yourself. Recall those good feelings, the situation surrounding them, and how you arrived at that place in your life. Try to remember how you carried yourself then and how your body language looked.

Remember that you are not out on a date to prove yourself.

You are not trying to demonstrate you are good enough for him. Rather, you are going out to decide whether *he* is good enough for *you*.

Don't be afraid of silences. Your goal is to appear calm, confident, and friendly. Remind yourself that you don't need to fill every moment of the evening with conversation. When pauses occur, don't fill the space with every detail of your life. If he wants to know more, he can ask you out again.

Make a conscious effort to talk slowly and in a low voice. This is especially important if your voice gets high and you begin talking faster when you feel nervous.

Remember your sense of humor. Confident people are able to laugh off minor inconveniences that may come up during a date rather than act distraught and make an issue of them.

Watch your body language. Don't slouch in your chair, play with your food, or avoid eye contact. Sit up straight and gaze into his eyes. If you're attracted to him, touch him on the sleeve or arm while making conversation.

Typical Dating Questions

Who pays on a dinner date? Traditionally, the man pays. Many women feel guilty for not paying but awkward when they do. Work out whatever arrangement you prefer. If you don't pay, treat him every third date or so with something special. Cook his favorite foods, take him to the theater, or walk his dog when he's out of town. When his birthday comes around, buy him something that will remind him of you often, a new telephone, answering machine, or personalized license plate. However, avoid spending too much money on a man you've just begun dating or you will make him feel obligated and uncomfortable.

Some women prefer going out with men who expect them to pay. The arrangement makes them feel less obligated to do anything other than what is planned. Other women feel this approach is less traditional, less romantic, and a lot less fun than being wined and dined.

What does it mean when a man says he'll call you? Never believe a man when he says, "I'll call you." It is synonymous with saying goodnight and good-bye. When he says this he is merely using a social courtesy, much like saying "excuse me," "thank you," or "you are welcome." The statement does not assure that he will call, but it does not mean he won't either. A good rule of thumb is not to believe any promises a man makes to you about the future of your relationship the first 48 hours that you know him.

Why doesn't he call? Sometimes a man may actually have intended to call but got distracted by other women. It's possible that you're just not his type. Or perhaps you're so much his type you remind him of a former wife or girlfriend who made his life miserable. Perhaps he intended to call at first but later decided against it. Don't lose confidence. Get on with meeting men who will appreciate you immediately.

Tips for Maintaining Self-Esteem While Dating

All he talks about is his work and you are so bored you wish you were at home watching TV. Don't sit there silently suffering. Try to change the subject. If he keeps going back to his work, say something like, "I hope you don't mind, but I'd rather hear more about what you do after hours than from nine to five."

He asks you out to an expensive restaurant and when the bill comes, he says he thought you knew you were going Dutch. You didn't know and wouldn't have ordered the lobster if you had. Don't sit there steaming. Tell him he should have been considerate enough to tell you ahead of time. Then, either pay half the bill if you're sure it was a misunderstanding, or else offer to treat him next time (at a place closer to your price range).

You go out to dinner with him and he embarrasses you by creating a scene when the service is bad. Remind him that the most effective way of demonstrating his disapproval is by not leaving a tip and that if he makes another comment, you're leaving. If he does, calmly get up and walk out.

Always give yourself permission to walk out if your date is acting like a jerk. Bring along cab fare so you can leave at any time. Or plan on taking separate cars (especially if you don't know him that well). Don't prolong the pain of a total dating disaster. Get up and walk out.

Dating and Sex

Don't sleep with a man until you've emotionally bonded with him. If there is any doubt in your mind about whether or not he'll call you again, it's too soon. It's difficult for you to bond emotionally before the fifth or sixth date and many women are waiting much longer. If he gets impatient, tell him you're worth waiting for. In the past you may have slept with men for all the wrong reasons. Dating Smart means that from now on you sleep with a man for all the right reasons.

Here are right reasons for sleeping with a man.

- Because *you* want to, not because he wants to. Sex is at its best when the feeling is mutual.

- Because you feel physically and emotionally safe with him. You've grown close enough to him to feel secure.

- Because he has many qualities you would value in a mate. You've been taking notes.

- Because you don't think of him as a "fantasy lover," but as a real person with both good and bad traits you recognize and believe you can accept in a long-term mate.

Many women have told me their sexual curiosity about a man always does them in. When they're attracted to a man, they want to know what he'll be like right away. But when you are looking for a marriage partner, you're not on a mission to indulge your sexual fantasies.

Maintaining perspective is so important for effective Romance Management. If you have to, tattoo your nonnegotiable needs on your kneecaps. It will be better for both of you if you learn to savor the anticipation. If you'd like to avoid the temptation of sleeping with a man too soon, consider these delaying tactics.

- Don't drink heavily on dates. Drinking distorts your judgment.

- Avoid spending unstructured time together. Plan your dates and involve yourselves in an activity you both enjoy. That way he won't feel obligated to press for sex to occupy open spaces of time.

- Exercise. Get rid of excess sexual energy with a good workout. You'll look better and feel more relaxed.

- Pamper yourself. Indulge in a massage or a facial, relax in a sauna or a hot tub.

Here are wrong reasons for sleeping with a man.

- To see what it would be like. One thing is sure, if you wait it'll be better.

- To keep him from dating other women. No matter how great it is, one night will not make a man monogamous.

- So things would seem more certain. If anything, jumping into bed too soon will have the opposite effect.

- To try and forget about someone else. Don't use sex as an escape.

- Because he kept pushing for it. Don't be talked into mercy sex. Just say no.

Acting in Your Own Best Interest Sexually

The Romance Management approach is all about acting in your own best interest, and practicing safe sex is an important part of the process. No one is immune to AIDS or any other communicable disease. Be prepared to practice safe sex by carrying condoms. This is not the time to forget that you're responsible not only for your love life, but your health as well. Don't play sexual Russian roulette just because condoms don't seem romantic. You can press the issue if you need to, but chances are he'll be aware of the risks and willing to comply. The Romance Management principal of "acting as if" comes in handy when you deal with this potentially awkward subject. He'll most likely follow your lead, so take an upbeat approach to the subject rather than a serious, clinical one. Avoid an awkward moment by keeping the condom handy so you won't be searching for it in a frenzy and feeling tempted to let it go this time. If you are casual about safe sex—especially the first time—you may have a hard time convincing him to cooperate later since you failed to set the proper ground rules.

Women have different approaches that work for them. The important thing is to remember, whatever your style, you need to practice safe sex.

Angela felt awkward the first time she had to assume a man felt the same way she did about the importance of safe sex, but "acting as if" worked so well she's no longer "acting."

I knew that we were going to sleep together that night. It just felt right. We'd gone out a month and I was ready. I even made the first move! We were having a candle-lit dinner at his place. After moving from the dining room to the bedroom before the main course, I just slowly pulled it out and whispered, "I'll help you put this on." I think because I made it part of the foreplay he didn't have the time or inclination to object. My approach is that there isn't a discussion about the issue, it's safe sex or no sex and that's my attitude.

Talking about the issue of safe sex before you get to the bedroom is a good way to avoid any unpleasant surprises. Avoid getting into a debate on the topic. Instead, offer a statement regarding your views on the subject and then act accordingly. Use the mantalk approach while "acting as if" to get the message across most effectively.

Roxanne, a 29-year-old hair colorist in a trendy hair salon in Marin county, decided to set limits on the safe sex issue, especially since her last sexual involvement hadn't lasted that long and she was beginning to become concerned about her health. With the last man she dated, Roxanne had had a long nonproductive argument about the importance of safe sex. Finally she just backed down, partly out of fear of losing the man and partly because he had finally "convinced" her she was being unreasonable. Afterwards she realized it wasn't just safe sex they were arguing about but the balance of power in the relationship. Even though she had assured him that once they got to know each other better they could reassess the situation, he still wasn't willing to compromise.

> The fact that I went along with it and didn't say no really makes me mad when I look back on it. Especially since he was as inconsiderate out of bed as in and we didn't even stay together that long. I started using the "acting as if" approach—which worked wonders and now I no longer "act as if." I really do expect a man to respect my wishes. Otherwise I assume he'll be selfish and uncompromising in bed too—so why should I risk my health to sleep with him?"

Roxanne shared with me the conversation she had with Andrew, her current boyfriend, with whom she is now in a monogamous relationship. At the time they were on their third date.

Roxanne: Did you read the article about AIDS in *Time* magazine this week?

Andrew: I read parts of it.

Roxanne: I had a friend who died of AIDs last year, a blood transfusion.

Andrew: I've known a few gay people I work with to come down with it though none of them have died yet. I still tend to think of it as a homosexual disease, not really effecting the straight community.

Roxanne: I use to think that way too (getting into agreement), but now I don't like to take chances. Safe sex isn't an issue I'm willing to compromise on (mantalk). You see, if I didn't practice safe sex, I'd probably be too uptight to enjoy it anyway (breaking the ice with humor).

Andrew: Well, in that case! (laughing)

Roxanne let Andrew know where she stood on the issue of safe sex in the beginning, so that if it was going to be an issue between them, she'd know before she got too involved with him. Two months later, after they'd been dating steadily and had shared their sexual histories and developed more trust between them, they became sexually intimate. Andy had been resistant to the idea of using a condom at first, but after he got to know Roxanne better and began caring more about her well-being, he didn't feel the need to insist on having things his way. Roxanne felt Andrew's willingness to practice safe sex was important and proved his feelings were beyond the superficial. Her decision to become intimately involved with him was reinforced by his actions and she was glad she'd finally learned to act in her own best interest.

When you sleep with a man the first time, take care to deal with minor details ahead of time so that later you won't be distracted. Decide, for instance, whether you plan to sleep at his place or yours. Though it doesn't sound very spontaneous, a little planning can make your first night together more enjoyable. After all, what's so romantic about a cluttered bedroom, dirty sheets, and no clean towels? Romance requires a little forethought. Don't be coy.

Be prepared. There is nothing worse than realizing in a moment of passion that you forgot your contact lens case, or worse, your diaphragm. Be honest with yourself about when your sexual involvement is likely to happen. You can be spontaneous and still be prepared. Carry a small, discreet make-up bag filled with all that you'll need.

To create the right mood at your place:

• Clear out all prescription drugs from sight.

- Turn on your answering machine, turn down the volume of your phone, and don't monitor your calls while he's there.

- Set out a pretty bouquet of flowers. Men like flowers as much as women do and they add a sensuous, romantic feeling to any environment. Don't wait for a man to bring you flowers, purchase them yourself. Let him wonder where they came from.

- Have snacks available. Don't turn into Suzy homemaker and bake his favorite cake, but have a few edibles on hand to munch in the middle of the night. If you don't think he's worth a little cheese and some crackers, you probably shouldn't let him sleep over.

- Don't surprise him. If you snore, talk in your sleep, or get up at dawn to jog, let him know about it rather than letting him wake up surprised. It could make a difference between his being amused or annoyed.

The morning after.

- Don't allow yourself to feel abandoned the morning after. Get up early and be frisky, but also have plans to meet a friend. Get dressed and get going, rather than hanging around home alone. If you spent the night at his place, don't wait for him to ask you to spend the day with him. By getting out early, he'll wonder if the night before was only a dream.

- If you're at his place, don't answer his phone, read his mail, ask who he talked to if he answers the phone, or look through his drawers. If you notice anything strange, make note of it but don't begin cross-examining him.

- Don't offer to make him an elaborate breakfast if he spent the night at your place. Save this for a little later. For now, you might want to surprise him with fresh orange juice or a cup of coffee and then send him on his way with a kiss.

COMPILING HIS PERSONALITY PROFILE

When I began to go out with the goal of finding a mate, my knowledge of my non-negotiable needs helped me break out of the eternal dating cycle. In the past I wasn't aware of my non-negotiable needs on a conscious level. Once I had actually taken the time to write them down, they became more real to me and the possibility of meeting a man who could satisfy them suddenly seemed possible.

Beginning at my first coffee-date interviews with the seven candidates I choose from the men who answered my ad, I took my non-negotiable needs into consideration. I realized that doing so didn't seem romantic, but I decided to worry about romance later, after I was in a relationship. After one divorce and several dead-end relationships, I was ready to take the pain and guesswork out of dating. At this point in my life, I'd developed clear preferances about what I was hoping to find in a mate. I was aware of my past pattern, that I was drawn to the men who were my total opposite. I was intrigued by the unknown, but major differences inevitably led to conflicts. I decided I'd dated enough different men to satisfy my curiosity forever. Now, however, I *had thought* about what I wanted. I was *not* looking for an adventure. I was searching for was a man who had marriage potential—one who was ready, willing, and able to satisfy my non-negotiable needs. I was seeking a man who shared similar interests, values, and outlook on the world. My ideal mate would be: emotionally stable, possess a good sense of humour, be fit and health-conscious, sexually compatible, willing to commit, steadily employed, and share my values and outlook on life.

During my interviewing process, for the first time I took a man's words to heart. I believed him when he said he didn't want to get married. Because I now had several men to choose from, I no longer wanted to convince a man of anything or to win him over to my way of thinking. I didn't say these things out loud. Had I confessed to each man that I was analyzing his potential to be my husband, he probably would have excused himself and disappeared.

I realized it wasn't enough to be aware of my non-negotiable needs. I also needed to be able to evaluate whether or not a particular man would be able to satisfy them. In order to make

an intelligent decision in the most time-efficient manner, I designed
a personality profile sheet for each man. As I began dating men
from my ad, I compiled information from them about their romantic potential and used it to expediate the process of screening
men in and out of my life. In addition to satisfying my non-
negotiables, I knew the chemistry between us would have to be
right. After choosing seven candidates from the men who responded to my ad, I began the process of gathering information
and assessing each man's romantic potential in regard to my non-
negotiable needs. Within three months after placing my ad, I had
met, dated, and screened through several men. Each man I met
had his merits. However, I quickly narrowed the field to three.
Neal, the man I married, is a physician who had always browsed
the personals and had finally decided to respond to two ads. He
had broken up with someone recently and decided to try the ads
because he was a busy physician who didn't like the complications
involved in dating people at his hospital.

When he read my ad he decided he wanted to meet me, so
he immediately sent a letter. He responded to another ad as well,
but because I screened through my ads more efficiently, we began
dating first. Years later I discovered the "other woman" whose
ad Neal responded to was someone I knew! When I met Neal I
was sure he was everything I was looking for and I couldn't
believe my luck in having it all happen with my first ad. He was
my type physically, had a sophisticated sense of humor (which
is so hard to find), our chemistry was electrical, and we both
enjoyed the same things. I was cautious, however. I continued
the date two other men who had marriage potential until Neal
and I decided to date exclusively. That occurred two months after
we met. As we got to know each other more intimately, I was
convinced, as he was, that we were meant for each other. We
were married a year after we met. When people meet they still
can't believe we met through the personals and that Neal was a
"mail order" husband!

Your Non-Negotiables

Forgetting to review your non-negotiable needs while dating
is similar to going on a diet without a calorie counter. If you are

hungry enough, chocolate cake will seem dietetic. Taking a personality profile of your man serves as your emotional "calorie counter." It requires that you make a conscious effort to listen and take mental notes to learn if he fits *your* bill for a potential mate. As soon as you begin getting to know him, start filling out the Personality Profile worksheet. Ideally, you should add to the profile each time you see him. Valuable information can't help you if it's stored in your short-term memory bank. It's easy to conveniently "forget" a valuable piece of information, like the fact that he's had a vasectomy, or doesn't believe in marriage, or is presently living with someone. If he is worth dating, he's worth documenting. Don't be lazy when it comes to your love life. Get the facts before making a decision. And always refer back to your non-negotiable needs.

During the first few dates, a man will spend a great deal of time telling you about himself. He will talk about his past in terms of his family, his career, and his success. He will speak of the future in terms of what his hopes and dreams are. Not only is what a man tells you important, but what he fails to mention is also worth noting. A man may have an area of his life that he refuses to discuss. You must respect his privacy. But if there are too many gaps in his story, and you're having a hard time getting a good reading on him, he may be hiding something.

It's important that you don't screen out a man prematurely. Make a note of things that bother you, but don't stop seeing him. Continue gathering information to decide if your initial impression about those matters was right. Check to see if you have misread or overreacted.

Will you make it as a couple? His personality profile will tell. You can't judge by any one area alone. Consider the entire picture before assessing his potential for a future with you. Though opposites do attract, the more similar you are, the more compatible you will be.

The Personality Profile begins with relatively straightforward information about the man's age, race, religion, level of education and marital status.

Religion

Nancy, an attractive 42-year-old clothing designer, told me her number-one non-negotiable need was that a man be a Chris-

PERSONALITY PROFILE

Name _____

Age _____

Race _____

Religion _____

Education _____

Marital status _____

Number of dependents _____

EXTERNALS THAT SHAPE YOUR LIVES TOGETHER

Career

- career, success, past, present _____
- career satisfaction? _____
- long term goals, dreams _____
- hours per week? _____
- flexibility? _____
- travel? _____
- high stress? _____

Social history

- social/leisure activities _____
- does he prefer groups or one-on-one? _____
- does he enjoy time alone? _____
- sports _____
- hobbies _____

Family patterns

- birth order _____
- how did the family show appreciation/fight? _____
- duties and responsibilities of mom and dad _____
- relationship with mom and dad _____
- current relationship _____
- socio-economic background _____

PERSONALITY PROFILE

(continued)

Internal functioning

- is he emotionally stable? _____
- what does he like/dislike about himself? _____
- how does he handle anger? _____
    - sulker _____
    - passive/aggressive _____
    - confrontive _____
    - violent _____
    - holds it in _____
    - withholds sex _____
    - silent treatment _____
- how does he handle positive feelings? _____
- what upsets him? _____
- what is he looking for in a mate? _____

Individual characteristics (lifestyle/money/habits)

Functioning in a relationship (his track record)

- how long do his relationships last? _____
- how have they ended? _____
- who left? _____
- what are his complaints about the women in his past? _____
_____
- was he faithful? _____
- what has been his "type"? _____
- how was money handled? _____
- are they now friends? _____

Sexual style (frequency/timing/attitudes)

Belief systems that effect compatibility

- political/religious views _____
- ethical/moral stance _____

tian like herself. At the time, however, she was dating a man who was a Moslem. Though she claimed she wanted to marry, Nancy had a pattern of getting involved with men of different religions whom she didn't consider "marriageable."

If religion is an important consideration to a woman, dating men of other religions is a sign of ambivalence about long-term relationships. Most of the time, however, people fall into relationships with people of different religions because they are compatible in all other areas and don't consider religion to be a divisive issue. At first it usually isn't.

Intermarriage between Jews and Christians is on the rise. About 40 percent of Jews and 45 percent of Catholics are marrying outside their faith. The success of intermarriage depends upon the ability of one member of the couple to convert or of both to accept the other's religion and compromise. Even so the issue of how to raise children can often be a source of later tension, especially if grandparents take a strong stand on religious issues. Religious heritage affects far more than one's moral code, so it is particularly important for couples of different faiths to examine carefully their attitudes about a wide array of issues.

The ability of couples to adapt to each other's religion is determined by the compatibility of their moral code, their lifestyle preferences, and their interests. Many couples find that their different religions enrich their own sense of history together and allow them to share a different outlook and perspective on life.

Education

Some people make the mistake of equating intelligence with academic degrees. It's understandable that you should desire a mate who matches your intelligence level, otherwise you may become bored and dissatisfied. However, don't judge a man by the number of degrees he's earned or the number of schools he's attended. Instead, notice the way he communicates his thoughts, the way he reasons and analyzes. If he is able to stimulate you intellectually and converse on a variety of topics, you should bear that in mind. College or high school grades don't tell the whole story.

Consider your own education level. The better educated you

are, the more career opportunities you'll have and the more appealing you will appear as a potential mate. If your level of education is higher than his, don't be tempted to "educate" him into being someone he's not. Either accept him as he is or move on. If you are less educated than a man you are dating, avoid acting insecure about it. Remember that basic intelligence has little to do with how much schooling you have had and more with the way you function in the world.

Consider the following questions.

Does he wish to return to school? If he wishes to return to school, you'll need to know about it before you marry because it will affect your lifestyle and plans for the future. You may have to put off having children and support him financially until he completes his education.

If you wish to return to school, he has a right to know as well. If you have been considering going back to school, don't wait until you marry to start fulfilling your desires. Begin now by attending evening classes and start acquiring credits.

Are you comfortable with his level of education? Are you bothered by the fact that you don't share the same amount of education? If so, are you worried what other people (your friends or family) will think? Or have you always assumed you'd marry someone with a similar educational background? If a difference in levels of education makes him less desirable, you'll either have to overcome your feelings or find someone closer to your ideal.

If he is presently in school, how much longer will it be until he finishes? If he just began his first year of medical school, for instance, you're in a much different situation than you would be if he was finishing his residency. School is very stressful for couples and many divorce during or immediately following completion of school. You may want to postpone marriage until he has completed his education.

Marital Status

How available for a long-term commitment is the man you dating?

Married but separated. A married man, even if he is living apart from his wife is not very eligible. He may go back to his wife. If he doesn't, and if he and his wife do divorce, he is about to face a great deal of pain, frustration, and guilt during the proceedings. The last thing he can think about seriously is remarriage, although most men do remarry within three to four years. Give him a chance to work through his problems, and date around a bit before hoping for anything permanent with him.

Separated and waiting for the divorce. A man in the process of divorce is still sorting his life out. If he has children, keep in mind that he must provide for them. Consider whether or not his wife is working. Remember, if you marry him, you take on his financial obligations. He may be bitter and angry at women in general and begin venting that resentment on you. It's best to wait until his life has stabilized before becoming involved.

Involved in common law arrangement, with children. Common law marriages are recognized in most states and you should recognize this as a significant commitment on his part. Many men who resist the idea of marriage fall into common law arrangements. Don't consider a man single and available if he is still living with a woman, especially if children are involved.

Divorced men. Men are sometimes reluctant to discuss their divorces, and in the beginning you should respect the need for privacy. Eventually, however, you need to know some of the details. Use these questions to determine how available for a new relationship a divorced man is.

How long has he been divorced?

Is he still bitter over the divorce?

Is he financially able to remarry and assist in supporting a new family if you wish to have children of your own?

If he has children, are you willing to co-parent?

If you have children, is he willing to co-parent?

ROMANCE MANAGEMENT WORKSHEET

AVAILABILITY CHART

MARRIED WITH CHILDREN	MARRIED WITHOUT CHILDREN	LONG TERM LIVING ARRANGEMENTS	SEPARATED	DIVORCED	SINGLE
FORGET IT!	• Divorce rate higher among childless couples however, • Childless couples rate higher on overall marital satisfaction than do couples with children	• Absence of marriage could mean reflection of life philosophy • unresolved problems • legal or financial problems	• still legally married • often emotionally unstable • sometimes go back	• How long? • Median remarriage time is 44 months after divorce • Financial issues • Child support? Alimony? • Are you available to co-parent? • If you have children would you want to bring a new family member into their lives? • Bitterness over divorce?	• If dating others you need to assess how entangled he is • Investment of time is a good indication of availability • History of long term relationships is a good sign

WATCH OUT FOR . . .

Psychologically unavailable men:

Married to their work

Responsibilities towards elderly parents

Professional bachelor/playboy

45, never married

If you both have children, do both you and your families feel positive about bringing the two families together?

Do either of you want a child over the other's wishes?

The unconfirmed confirmed bachelor. Yes, there are exceptions, but if he is 45 and has never been married, it is unlikely that he ever will. You know the one. He's gorgeous, well-off, and still single after all these years. Often this type will be very passive. He rarely has to pursue because he's always being pursued. Unless you want to grow grey waiting for this one, forget him.

The Availability Chart on p. 136 sets out schematically questions of availability for every category of marital status.

Career

Never underestimate the importance of a man's career. Until he has achieved a certain amount of success, he may be reluctant to marry. Moreover, his career is worth considering in the long run since it will affect the quality of your life. His career is especially important if you plan to have children and hope to stay home or work part-time. His career will dictate the amount of time you spend together and how much responsibility he will be able to assume in areas such as child-rearing and household management.

Career transitions can be extremely stressful to couples, especially if further education, which can be lengthy and costly, is required. Know how a man feels about his career. If he wants to change, you may both decide to wait until he has successfully done so before embarking on marriage and a family.

Examine his long-term dreams and determine if they will mesh with yours. For instance, if he hopes to pursue life as a rock musician, traveling around the country on tour, will you be willing to sacrifice being together a good part of the time so that he may follow his dream?

If his job is a high-powered one and includes a great deal of travel, stress, and political socializing, will he expect you to put your career on the back burner? If so, would you be willing to do so without feeling neglected and resentful?

Most men have a personal agenda they must accomplish in

regard to their career before they feel ready to settle down and marry. Don't overlook his need to prove himself before he feels complete. Try to gauge how far he is from satisfying his life goals.

Consider whether he is a "dreamer," or whether he has a good chance of realizing his career goals. Does he have a history of setting goals and then accomplishing them or does he fail to follow through?

Ask yourself the following questions.

Is he required to travel a lot? Will he always?

Is he a workaholic?

Is he happy with his career or will he eventually want to change jobs?

Does he always work late?

Does he have a future?

Does he respect my career?

If we have children, what does he expect I will do about my job? What do I expect him to do?

Leisure Time Preferences

How a man prefers to spend his leisure time will make a great difference in your life together. How does his preferred form—groups or one-on-one—mesh with yours? Can you enjoy the same sports or hobbies?

Family Influences

We're all influenced somewhat by our childhood experiences. Our families teach us a lot about love, intimacy, and marriage. Consider what kind of messages he received from his parents. Consider also his family's particular style of communication and whether or not it is similar to the style you grew up with.

Lauren and David's differences in upbringing threatened to

cause major problems in their relationship. Lauren came from a
quiet, conservative background. When problems arose, the family
discussed them calmly and strictly within the family. Since her
father was in politics, her parents were concerned about what
other people thought and constantly coached Lauren as to what
she should and shouldn't repeat to others. In contrast, David's
family gossiped a great deal and criticized and made fun of each
other a lot, especially at meal times. When Lauren and David
spent time with both of their families on Thanksgiving, the source
of their differences became apparent.

> I thought David was always picking on me but I can
> see now that it's a form of affection that his whole
> family shares. My family sweeps everything under the
> rug while his lays it right out on the dining room table.
> I think I could benefit some from opening up a little,
> but I'll never feel comfortable having our personal life
> discussed over dinner by his family. My parents would
> never dream of asking point blank, "So when are you
> getting married?" Yet this was one of the first things
> out of his mother's mouth after we met.
>
> We are making an attempt now to compromise and
> develop a style of communication with each other and
> our families that works. This means that David doesn't
> share every intimate detail of our life with his family
> or tease and criticize me in front of them. It also means
> that I open up with him rather than keep secrets and
> quit trying to maintain a facade of having the perfect
> relationship because I'm so concerned about what other
> people think.

Other things to be aware of regarding his family include the
following.

His relationship with his mother. If a man is close to his
mother while retaining his independence from her, it is a good
sign. His earliest impressions about women were formed by the
impression he had of his mother. Find out what kinds of emotions
she evokes in him.

Male role models and mentors. Role models that a man grew

up with may lay dormant until years later when he marries or
has a child and then they begin slowly to surface. Take a look
at who served as a role model to him while he was growing up.

Physical or psychological abuse in his family. Be aware of any
abuse patterns in his family. These often repeat themselves and
you need to watch out for them.

His feelings about his family. How does he speak of his family?
Are they close or have they not spoken in years?

His parents' relationship to each other. Do his parents play
traditional roles? Did his father make all the decisions in the
family when he was growing up and did his mother "obey"? If
so, you may have to bring about some changes before you can
live with him.

Emotional Stability

These characteristics concern the man as an individual. Is
he emotionally stable? How does he feel about himself? How
does he express anger? How does he express other emotions?
What upsets him? And what sort of woman is he looking for?
The answers to these questions will tell you whether he is someone
you can live with day in and day out for a long time.

Individual Characteristics

Lifestyle

As you get to know each other, you will both be considering
how well you fit into each other's future plans. It's important to
discuss the kind of lifestyle you're both looking for and consider
it in the overall scheme of things. Here are some questions to
consider.

Would he expect you to quit your job and stay home if you have
children?

Does he feel his career comes first?

Do you enjoy spending your free time together pursuing leisure

activities or do you find your interests are so different you have
little in common?

Is he outgoing or quiet, somewhere in between?

Money

Differences in the way people spend, save, and invest can
cause a great deal of conflict. In addition, power plays involving
money are quite common in relationships and, not surprisingly,
the person with the higher income most often has the most clout.
Your financial approaches may differ from his because of the
way your families handled money and because of your long-term
goals and plans. His past marital status and whether or not he
has children also can affect the financial dynamics between you.

As in other areas of your life, your upbringing has a great
deal to do with your financial outlook.

Cecelia, a 34-year-old speech pathologist, never bothered to
balance her checkbook or to open a savings account. Her approach
to finances was learned from her parents, who were totally irresponsible financially and, though they both had good incomes,
were not even able to save for their retirement or buy their own
home. Tim, a 36-year-old accountant, was Cecelia's opposite.
Raised in a frugal household, his mother was the money manager.
Although his father earned little money, all five of his brothers
and sisters were provided for and educated.

After dating a few months and sharing expenses, the differences in the way they handled money began to surface and
cause concern between them. Initially they both joked about each
other's spending style. However, during a vacation they took to
Paris, money became an issue between them. After a long day
of sightseeing, Cecelia suggested that they catch a cab back to
the hotel rather than walk because she was so tired. Tim objected
because of the cost and suggested they walk at least part of the
way to save money. Exhausted and irritated, Cecelia told Tim
she wasn't about to start pinching pennies in Paris, and if he
wanted to he could walk, but she was riding.

Cecelia realized her approach to finances was out of control
and she wanted a mate who had a better sense of how to provide
for the future than she did. However, she felt that Tim's approach

of always saving and forever delaying gratification was too self-sacrificing. Tim realized he was too uptight when it came to spending money and that he wanted a mate who could help him loosen up and enjoy spending money. However, he felt Cecelia was too extravagant and irresponsible with money. Though they were in love with each other and wanted to marry, they realized they had to first work out their financial differences.

Since financial security was important to both of them, they drew up a budget, and both contributed to pay for expenses. A certain amount remained Cecelia's "mad money," which she was not obligated to account for. Tim had his own mad money, and, with Cecelia's encouragement, he was able to spend more freely and enjoy it more than in the past.

Cecelia and Tim had serious financial differences, but by being aware of them and working them out in advance, they didn't allow their differences to ruin their marriage.

Here are some money matters to watch out for.

Does he always make an issue of how much an evening out costs? If so, he may be a money monger. Separate finances are a must if you marry a money monger. Otherwise, he'll expect a receipt for every purchase you make with his money.

Does he seem to be extravagant about the way he spends money? Is he always showering you with gifts? Delightful. But once you marry the generous type, you end up sharing the cost of his expensive tastes. If he can afford to be generous, fine. If not, you'll end up sharing his financial obligations.

Does he think he can buy you? If he's generous but expects too much in return for a few gifts and dinner, tell him that if he's trying to make you feel obligated, it's not working. Any man who feels he can win you over with material possessions is usually trying to compensate for personality deficiencies. Be wary.

If it's not obvious how he handles money, a good way to learn is to ask him for pointers on financial issues. The extent of his financial savvy will usually influence his personal habits as well.

Habit Patterns

Initially, it's easy to overlook irritating habits in a man who interests you. Often the very things that attracted you to him in the beginning may later drive you crazy. For instance, organizational habits may seem trivial or even cute while you are dating. However, once you begin sharing a life together, major differences in your habits can pose a threat to your mental health and the longevity of your relationship.

Mark, a 41-year-old jeweler, was meticulous about the way he kept his surroundings, to the point that he color-coded his closet and alphabetized his record collection. Angie, a 39-year-old photographer, was creative and liked to see the whole picture, rather than get hung up on details. Her existence was totally disorganized and chaotic. Mark and Angie often joked about their differences. Angie even photographed Mark in his color-coded closet and mounted it in her closet to inspire herself to hang up her clothes. Mark was attracted to Angie's free spirit and unorganized lifestyle because it was so much unlike his own. He found himself spending more of his free time at her place and enjoying it, despite the fact that he continued to be as neat and organized as ever at home. After dating a year, they decided to marry. They bought a condo together and soon realized the differences which had amused and attracted them to each other initially were impossible to live with. Mark's compulsive neatness may have been cute at a distance, but day to day it drove Angie crazy, especially when he suddenly expected her to be a neatnik too. Eventually they compromised. Mark lowered his standard of organization and cleanliness a bit and Angie raised hers. In addition, they hired a housekeeper to come in once a week.

Wendy, a 34-year-old department store buyer, and Rob, a 40-year-old engineer, had a temperature conflict. Rob liked to sleep with the windows wide open year round. Wendy was always cold and usually slept with an electric blanket on high. At first they both joked about it and each compromised. Rob opened the windows only halfway and Wendy turned her blanket down to medium. Soon, however, Rob complained that he woke up sweating and that Wendy was more attached to her blanket than she was to him. Wendy even had her blood iron levels checked, hoping that was the reason she always felt cold. When her checkup revealed nothing wrong, Wendy tried to ease the situation by purchasing a new blanket with dual controls that would allow Rob to keep his side of the bed as cool as he liked. Things still didn't work out. Eventually Wendy got tired of hearing Rob complain about her blanket so she broke off the relationship.

Other seemingly trivial but later serious habits include the following.

Tardiness. Is he always late? You may be willing to overlook it now, but can you handle being married to someone who never shows up for anything on time and resents your complaining about it?

Forgetfulness. Does he constantly lose things? A man who always misplaces car keys, income tax returns, his checkbook, or a credit card may need a personal valet more than a wife.

Procrastination. Does he put off until tomorrow . . . ? Procrastinating is a terrible habit. Imagine if you always have to police him to do what he said he would do yesterday? You'd probably grow frustrated and wind up doing it all yourself, and that is not a good habit for you to develop.

Obsessive interests. Does he attend wrestling matches or watch every single sports wrap-up program? If so, can you live with it or do you think you can wean him off it?

Flakiness. Does he sometimes act spaced-out? Does he forget about meeting you and just not show up, or do you know you can always depend on him?

Boys' nights out. If going out with his friends is a weekly ritual, he'll undoubtedly intend to carry on the tradition once you tie the knot. How do you feel about it?

His Track Record

A man's romantic track record will provide you with some insight into his behavior around women, and it may reveal any set patterns he has which would be difficult to change. If he has a history of long-term relationships with women, it is a good sign. On the other hand, if he has never been in a committed relationship and seems to never have ever practiced monogamy, chances are he won't be any different with you.

What about a man who has never been monogamous before or wasn't ready to settle down but claims he is now? Knowledge of his track record is still important. It may alert you to potential areas of conflict that have been issues in his past relationships. Also, even if he thinks he is ready to change, knowing his track record allows you to decide whether or not you want to risk taking a chance with *him*. You gather information about his romantic track record by listening to what he says. Most people talk freely about their past relationships. Some men will even offer more than you want to know. The key to assessing his record is knowing what to listen for. The following questions will help you focus on important areas. In addition, watch for clues regarding his attitude and outlook on relationships in general. Remember, you should be filling out his personality profile from your first date and make a note of anything worth mentioning in your dating diary.

How long ago did his last relationship break up? If a man has broken up recently, he may be on the rebound. If he was married and has recently become separated or divorced, he is making a serious transition in his life. He may not be truly ready to commit to a new relationship even though he thinks he is.

What happened in his last relationship? Patterns have a way of repeating themselves in relationships. If you know the major issues in his past relationship, you can anticipate conflict that could resurface in those areas. For instance, if the last woman left because he wouldn't make a commitment, you need to know about it. Was it because he wasn't "ready," or because she wasn't "right"? If they fought because he wasn't attentive enough, worked too much, or spent too much time with the guys, your relationship may turn into a rerun of his last one. Was there another woman? If he is easily distracted by other women and doesn't stay in one relationship too long, don't fool yourself into believing you can be the one to change him.

Who broke it off? If she left him, he could still be suffering from the breakup and trying to recoup in his relationship with you. He shouldn't mourn forever. If her name comes up frequently, she's still on his mind. Don't play the therapist. Once he's told you the whole story and you know the score, tell him that you can continue to see him only if he is capable of letting her go.

If he left her, beware. He may be tempted to return. Ask how many times they've broken up before. If he has a history of breaking up and reuniting, proceed with caution, especially if he married, lived with, or otherwise was involved with her for a year or longer. A man who appears to be free may just be on a brief outing from his regular relationship and may return to safety as soon as things get too hot to handle with you.

What was his complaint about her? Listen to his major complaint about the last woman as well as previous women in his past. If he describes all women in his past as inconsiderate, selfish, mercenary, dull, needy, desperate, and demanding, warning bells should go off in your head. It's tempting to believe that he's made wrong choices in the past but now that he's met you everything is going to be different. Chances are, however, he's developed stereotypes about women and a tendency to generalize them according to his preconceived beliefs. You too may one day become just like all the rest.

This kind of stereotyping can occur in women as well. You should examine your own attitudes about men to see whether you too may operate with rigid stereotypical views.

Does he have a bad track record? If he has a bad track record, admits it, and says it's his fault, believe him, thank him for his honesty, and move on. Why take chances with a man who has a poor track record? You're not looking for a long shot, but a sure bet. You wouldn't gamble your savings in an investment that showed a poor rate of return, nor should you invest your emotions with a man who has a poor track record.

If it's challenge and excitement you are seeking, consider going on outward-bound adventures or try skydiving. Satisfy your desire for excitement, challenge, and adventure in a productive and positive way rather than in a destructive way by trying to win over a man who is emotionally unavailable for a relationship.

How long have his relationships lasted? Does he have a history of serial monogamy? If so, this is a good sign and shows that he is capable of a long-term involvement. This is true whether he lived with a woman, was married, or just dated. After the third or fourth date he will begin sharing details of what happened in these relationships. Areas to focus on include what drew him to her (how did she satisfy *his* non-negotiable needs), what caused friction between them (these conflicts often resurface), and what ultimately caused them to break up.

Is he on speaking terms with any of his former girlfriends? If not, investigate further. Speak with them personally if you get the chance. Quiz mutual friends who may have the inside story. Don't feel guilty about asking around. Your romantic future is worth a little investigative work. And if he has nothing to hide, why should it bother him? If he is annoyed by your snooping, use humor. Say something like, "It seems that after you broke up with the women in your past, they were never heard from again. I just wanted to make sure that if the same thing happened to us, I wouldn't end up somewhere in dating purgatory."

Sexual Style

Are you sexually compatible? Do you agree on the frequency and sexual style of your partner? Is he considerate and caring when you make love or only concerned about his own needs? Sex is an important part of your relationship. Don't ignore a man's inability to satisfy you. If he seems eager to please and willing to learn, take your time and teach him how to make you happy. Remember to offer him plenty of positive reinforcement. If he doesn't know how or care to please you, don't fool yourself into thinking that your sex life isn't that important and he has other qualities that can make up for it. And don't think that once you marry, your sex life will get better. You deserve a mutually satisfying sexual relationship with the person you marry. Don't settle for anything less.

Frequency. If your sex styles and drives are similar, and your preferred frequency is the same or close to his, you are sexually compatible. If, on the other hand, he requires sex quite a bit more often or less frequently than you do, you may not be compatible unless both of you are able to compromise. Your man will be difficult to get along with if he feels sexually deprived and you'll feel angry and resentful if he is constantly pressing for or backing away from sex. When one is always saying "no" sexually and the other always pressing for "yes," a power play begins which results in difficulties both in and outside the bedroom. In order to have a harmonious relationship, you need to find a man who has a similar sex drive.

Timing. One major difference between a casual relationship and serious courtship is the timing of sexual involvement. It will influence whether or not a man will consider you as a potential wife. Once a man makes an emotional investment in you, he is more likely to think of you as a love object than a sex object. It takes some time to learn about his sexual attitudes. If you sleep with him too soon for instance, and then learn he is sexually conservative, he may have enjoyed the experience but he may judge you harshly as a result of it.

Attitudes. While pacing your sexual involvement, listen for clues as to how he feels about sex in general. Is he uptight about sex or does he consider it healthy and natural? Does he seem embarrassed when there is a sex scene in a movie or does he enjoy it? Ask how affectionate his parents were when he was growing up. Listen to the way he describes his single women friends who are sexually active. Do you get the impression he thinks it's okay for women to have sex before marriage or not? How experienced would he want his wife to be? Men are attracted to women who are sexy and like sex, but they often don't want to marry a woman who they think has an extensive sexual history. Don't be tempted to tell all. You shouldn't lie about your sexual past, but you needn't give out intimate details either. Few men want to marry an inexperienced virgin, but neither do they want a sexual expert. Act in your own best interest by being modest when it comes to discussing your sexual past. It will be necessary to discuss your sexual histories somewhat in order to insure your safety in regards to AIDS and other sexually transmitted diseases. However, don't let him know how many men you've slept with in your life and don't offer up a description of each encounter.

When you become sexually involved, let him know you wish

to practice safe sex and make sure you're prepared to do so even if he isn't. If you've started having sex and your man tries to introduce any unusual sexual practices, don't give him the impression that you've done it all and that you're jaded. Enter into any new sexual adventure with him enthusiastically—as long as you enjoy it as well as he does.

Listening to Both His Words and His Actions

Even though you've been paying a lot of attention to his words, they are not the only source of information about him. Sometimes what he doesn't say or what he unintentionally brings up can be even more revealing than his more direct statements. Watch for any of the following diversionary tactics.

Joking rather than giving a straight answer. Men who joke about everything and can't handle a serious situation are scared of sharing their feelings. During the first date, it may be nerves. If on the second date he's still acting like a comic, consider him for what he's turning out to be: a form of entertainment.

Freudian slips. Laugh off Freudian slips, but don't forget them. If he calls you by another woman's name, he's thinking of her, not you. If he keeps it up, start calling him by a former boyfriend's name or begin concentrating on one of the other men in your life.

Changing the topic. He may not want to discuss intimate details of his life, but if he won't even tell you where he lives, you know he's being unnecessarily evasive.

Getting defensive. If a man seems to protest too much about anything in particular, make a note of it in your dating diary.

Generalizing about women. If, for example, he really believes his co-worker, a 35-year-old single woman, is "unstable" because she is divorced and raising her son alone, you better keep your ears open for more of the same. If he thinks his best friend's girlfriend is insensitive because she plans to keep her maiden name when they marry, he may be very traditional. How does that sit with you?

Before jumping to any permanent conclusions about things a man says, take into account the fact that he could be nervous. Give yourself some time to firm up your impressions. In order to do this, "file" the information for later assessment. Plan to refer back to your early notes as the relationship progresses to spot consistencies in his behavior. If he's not as defensive and elusive as he was in the beginning, you'll know it was just nerves at the time.

Actions

Always observe a man's actions as well as his words. How he behaves in certain situations will tell you more than an evening's worth of talk.

Situation: You have just finished brunch and are walking out of the restaurant when a mother walks by with a beautiful infant in a stroller. You comment on the beautiful child and ask him, "Would you like to have children someday?"

Reaction: Does he hesitate, stammer, or say nothing? If he reacts in any of these ways, he may either not want children now, or feel uncomfortable about your asking. Wait for the subject to come up again and then gauge his response.

If he automatically responds by saying he loves children and wants to have his own one day, you've got your answer. You can follow up and find out about his time line by asking something about what he would like to accomplish in life before having children. If he gets defensive and wants to know why you're asking, he's feeling scrutinized. Don't be put off. Compliment him by saying, "Well, I think you'd make an awfully good father."

Be prepared for him to turn the question back on you. Have an answer ready that doesn't sound as if all you want to do is get married and have babies, even if you do. You don't need to mention that you want six children and that you've already chosen their names. A simple "yes" will do.

Situation: You're walking down the street together and run into a woman he knows. He introduces her to you and she seems a little cool towards him. Is she a former or a current interest of his? You ask him, "How do you know her?"

Reaction: If he answers without hesitating and tells you they went to school together or are neighbors, believe him and drop it. If you press on, you'll sound insincere and jealous. Be patient and wait. If something else is going on with them, you'll have other opportunities to find out about it.

If he hesitates and seems flustered, she may be a former girlfriend or a current interest. Don't let him off the hook by changing the subject. If he seems vague about her, it's safe to assume they are seeing each other. Don't pry. Make a note of what he says about her in your dating diary and place a question mark next to his availability status. If you happen to run into the woman when you are alone, feel free to ask her point blank if they are dating. She'll probably tell you the truth, so why waste time wondering?

If he gets defensive and feels you are prying, defuse the situation with humor. Say something like, "Well, if I need to get a number and stand in line, I want to know about it." Say this in a lighthearted manner and then drop it. He'll get the message.

Situation: You go with him to a party at his friend's house where you don't know anyone. No one acts particularly friendly to you and then you overhear someone asking him if he's heard from his old girlfriend. You say, "I guess your friends are accustomed to seeing you with your ex-girlfriend. Are they hoping you might get back together?"

Reaction: If he admits that they do, say something like, "I can understand that, they probably got accustomed to you as a couple." Whatever you do, don't attack his friends or him because you feel rebuffed. You'll only alienate him. Don't try to win his friends over either. Just be yourself and they'll eventually come around to accepting you. Also realize that his friends may be reflecting his own ambivalence and he may very well have discussed with them the possibility of getting back together with his old girlfriend.

If he gets defensive, he may be feeling guilty about wanting to be with her instead of you, or he may feel you are prying. Either way, humor will work with this touchy topic. Say, "Well, I just wanted to know if it's really over or if you're just doing a comparison study." Drop the subject but notice his response.

AVOID PREMATURE DISCLOSURE

Disclosure is necessary to become intimate with a man but watch your timing. Recently I was on a radio talk show in San Francisco when a 37-year-old man called to get this off his chest.

Why is it that women are always baring their souls on dates? When I ask a woman out, I definitely want to get to know her better, her likes and dislikes, but it always turns into her talking about her problems and how depressed she is. Why can't they just relax and have a good time?

Dating is not a long-term one-on-one therapy. If you find yourself sharing all your personal, emotional, and financial problems during the first few dates with a man, and you're not paying him by the hour, you are confusing dating with therapy.

Disclosing too much personal information too soon may make a man uncomfortable because he feels he is supposed to disclose as well, and he may not want to. Don't confess something you don't feel good about in the hopes he'll accept you, warts and all. It may be a bit soon to hope for unconditional love from a man you just met. Wait until you've been dating a while before revealing information that places you in a less-than-flattering light. In other words, don't tell in order to test him.

Remember, while you are interviewing him, he is also interviewing you. So spotlight your assets, especially in the beginning of a relationship. You need to protect your privacy and maintain your self-esteem while getting to know someone new. If you don't tell too much too soon, you won't feel exposed if things don't work out, and he'll still be curious to hear more.

Even topics that you wouldn't consider off limits can send him the wrong messages about you. Avoid showing yourself in an unfavorable light by holding your tongue on the following.

"I can't control my kids." Focus on getting to know *him* before you begin confiding your child-rearing problems. Moreover, if you tell him that your children are difficult, he won't look forward to meeting them.

"I hate my job." You'll sound as if you are looking for a man to support you. Don't give him this wrong impression.

"I'm in therapy." Not everyone understands or accepts the benefits of therapy. He may think you're neurotic or have deep-seated problems. It's best to keep the state of your mental health to yourself.

Other topics to avoid bringing up until you're certain the relationship has potential are any health problems, details of your childhood, your parents' divorce, any income or financial problems, a past abortion, and so forth. There is, however, a time to tell.

Ellen, a 34-year-old nutritionist, told David, a man she'd been dating for six weeks, that she found him attractive and wanted to keep dating him but she thought he should know that she was unable to have children. She'd told him that was the reason she and her husband had gotten divorced. Sharing the secret was the only way Ellen could learn whether or not she and David had a future together. David was surprised at first but decided that if he and Ellen got married they could always adopt.

Ellen's revelation led to David's disclosure about his job. When they had first met, he had told Ellen he quit his job because he had been offered something better. The truth was he had been fired but at the time he didn't want to tell her because he was afraid she'd label him a "loser."

If David had been disappointed by Ellen's disclosure and never called her again, Ellen would then have known exactly where she stood with David and she wouldn't be wasting her time in a relationship that had no future.

Your Past Relationships

Your past relationships are bound to come up, especially since he'll be telling you similar information about himself. Even though you want him to be totally honest with you on this score, exercise some restraint yourself. Do not feel guilty about doing so. Remember, just as you'll be making judgments about his potential based on his past relationships, so he will be evaluating you. If you are to stay in control of the situation—and you are trying to do so—you have to gather more of this information early in the relationship. You'll have an opportunity later on to offer more details about your past relationships.

If you tell a man about all the other men in your past who have done you wrong, he may think you were at fault for being involved with such men in the first place. Or he may think you'll end up saying the same things about him one day. If he suspects you have a pattern of being attracted to the wrong type of man, he may feel not bother becoming involved with you further. So if you're asked about past relationships, simply say, "It didn't work out," "We grew apart," or "We both decided it wasn't working." This makes you sound in control of your life, an image you wish to convey.

If you bring up details from your very last relationship, he may get the impression you're still in love with that man. How would you feel if you were dating a man and all he could talk about was his old girlfriend? Even if he does act curious, don't tell all. Otherwise, you'll leave him too little to wonder about.

Do not attempt to remove all doubt and worry from a man's mind in regard to his competition. This is a major error. During your first few dates, never freely offer information about other men in your life. No man should be privy to that much information at such an early stage in your relationship. Until you have a better idea of how available he is, why offer privileged information? For all you know, he may be dating several other women. Never say that other men you're seeing are only friends, or you're not dating anyone special. Keep him guessing.

Only when your relationship has been firmly established should you disclose sensitive information about yourself. At this point such revelations can help you assess whether there is, in fact, a future for the two of you.

MEN WHO TEST YOUR LIMITS

Men enjoy playing games as much as women. Perhaps they like it even more, because they've been playing games since childhood. By testing your limits, men get a chance to see how much bad conduct on their part you'll put up with before you throw a tantrum. As a child, you called this game "Uncle" and would not scream that word until you were at the brink of excruciating pain. As an adult player, never reach that point, but scream "Uncle" early on. A man can test your limits in a variety of ways, including flirting with other women while you're out on a date, not introducing you to friends he meets on the street, and so forth.

Punctuality

One of the more common ways to test your limits is showing up late for dates. Don't let him get away with it—even if it occurs on the first date. Using humor as always, say something like, "You're on probation for being late, but I'll let you spend the rest of the night making up for it."

If a man is occasionally late, but is promising in every other way, never bawl him out. Instead, rise above the occasion.

After Neal and I were married, he became late for most everything. I would rant and rave about how late we were going to be to meet another couple, attend a party, or even catch a plane for our vacation. The more I complained, the less cooperative he was until I dreaded making plans to go out. Finally I decided to try a new approach. I quit allowing myself to be put in situations where I would have to suffer as a result of his chronic lateness. Since we both have our own cars, and I've never had a problem going places alone, I began leaving for my destination at the appropriate time, with or without him. Our friends are now accustomed to the arrangement and when he joins us late, we always say something like, "Glad you could make it!" I've found that since I gave up making Neal get ready on time, he's late a lot less often.

The Spanish Inquisition

A man may also test your limits by subjecting you to a barrage of leading questions. If you feel like your date is interrogating you, use humor to get him to back off. Say something like, "What are you planning to do, write my biography? Or throw him off course by saying, "Enough about me, now lets talk about you." *This should also serve to remind you to be discreet about how you gain information from him.*

Danger Signals

When you first meet a man, it's easy to overlook a lot of things, especially when the chemistry is right. That's why you need to be on the lookout for the following danger signals.

- He's still talking about his old girlfriend. If he does, he's still hung up on her. Don't nurse him through it. Tell him to call you in six months.

- He tries to sweep you off your feet. If he comes on too strong, he'll cool off quick. Don't be rushed.

- He's got problems and you spend all your time together talking about them. Don't be tempted to rescue him. Give him the name of a good therapist and move on.

- He spends several nights a week out with "the boys" bar hopping.

By taking gradual steps when you begin to date, and by exploring a man's character and history carefully, you can determine with some assurance the men who offer promise for the long term.

ROMANCE MANAGEMENT RULE #5:

Research a man in much the same way you would research a company you would consider purchasing.

ADVANCED DATING

Don't compromise yourself. You are all
you've got.

—JANIS JOPLIN

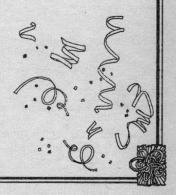

CONGRATULATIONS! You have gotten beyond the third date. There is obviously a mutual attraction between you and definite hope for the future. But you are both still dating, still seeing other people. Until you arrive at the point of mutual monogamous commitment you must remember to apply the principles of Romance Management toward building a relationship. Never lose sight of your romantic goals and whether he can satisfy them. At this delicate transitional stage, when you move from getting to know each other to becoming a couple, it is easy to forget your Romance Management principles and your common sense. Don't cease your efforts to consciously orchestrate your romance for long-term mutual benefit. Continue to act in your own best interests. Remember, repeated disappointments with men can permanently damage your self-esteem.

INVITING HIM OVER

After about your third date, you may want to invite him over to see your place. It's important for the two of you to start spending unstructured, quality time together in a home setting. When you invite him over, keep the following rules.

- Don't play hostess. Be nice, but show him around so he can help himself.

- Don't slide into the "let's order a pizza and rent a video" form of date at home. This is not the time for that yet. Create more exciting memories. Serve dinner by candlelight and listen to the stereo; play your favorite song.

- Make sure he's comfortable. Find out the kind of music he likes, his favorite wine. Surprise him with both when he arrives.

- Decide ahead of time if he's going to be sleeping over. Don't send any mixed messages about what the evening has in store for him. Otherwise, if he isn't staying you may have a hard time getting him out the door.

- Know enough about the work he does to carry on a conversation.

- Make your place clean and neat and cozy. A man will notice if your place is a mess.

- Find out ahead of time how he feels about pets. Many men don't like cats at all. If you have a cat, keep your kitty litter and cat food out of sight. Make sure your apartment doesn't smell. If he is allergic to cats, you may have to spend most of your time at his place. If you come to think the relationship has potential, you may want to offer to pay for his allergy shots.

- If you have young children, let him meet them briefly. Don't test him to play daddy. The first time he visits, you may want to hire a babysitter to entertain the children and then put them to bed. If your kids are difficult, keep them out of the picture altogether for a while. This is too soon to start testing his limits.

Although you want him to feel comfortable in your home, do not let him just drop by unannounced. He should not have visitation rights any time he happens to be in the neighborhood. If you let him do so, he'll begin taking your relationship for granted. If he does drop by without calling first, don't invite him in. Tell him you have company. Only the UPS man should be dropping by unannounced.

BE LOVE STINGY

Never confess your undying love for him right off, even if you think he is also smitten. It's not wise. Give him something to look forward to. By being unpredictable, you're once again using the powerful psychological tool called inconsistent positive reinforcement. You remember how successfully IPR can work with men you don't even care about that much. An occasional air of indifference makes men never want to give up. This does not mean you should play with a man's genuine affection or act insincerely. Such manipulative IPR can work great destruction. You want to avoid it from him, and he will certainly lose interest in you if he believes you are faking everything to satisfy your own private ends. No relationship will last very long without mutual trust and affection. You will practice IPR naturally if you express the full range of your emotions. You will find that you challenge him more if you insist on being yourself completely. Don't act "up" all the time if you don't feel that way. Your mood and outlook are always changing. Use them to your advantage.

Don't always be the one who is trying to make your relationship "work out." Back off and let him do some of the emotional work. That way he'll feel proud of the emotional investment he's made in you. Once he's invested in the relationship, he'll be less likely to drift away. You can build a relationship only if *both* of you construct it.

Camille, a 42-year-old attorney, was always anxious to smooth things out with Eric, her boyfriend, as she had with all the former men in her life. Whenever there was a fight or misunderstanding, Camille played the therapist, cleared the air, and got things back on track. The men in her life never had to express their emotions, work at keeping the relationship together, or fear any retribution for being inconsiderate of her needs. Camille was afraid that if she didn't straighten things out, the men in her life would leave her. Since they always had left her anyhow, she took a chance with Eric and decided to quit policing her relationships. Soon all hell broke loose because Eric was forced to examine his feelings and make an effort to communicate with Camille. As a result, he became more emotionally "connected" to her, and they grew beyond a superficial level into a deeper and more committed relationship. Had Eric left Camille, she would still have been better off. She could then look for a true relationship, one which had the active participation of *both* couple.

STAYING ON TRACK

It may have been easy for you to follow Romance Management initially, but now that you're falling in love and you believe the feeling is mutual, you may become a victim of lovesickness. Stick by your ground rules. Otherwise your self-esteem will suffer. Remember what drew him to you initially—the fact that you have a life of your own and varied interests. Don't make the mistake of dropping everything else in your life now and putting him at the center of your universe.

Don't allow him to become lackadaisical with regard to common courtesy. Let him know that becoming more familiar doesn't mean becoming less considerate. You still expect him to show up on time and treat you with consideration. If he doesn't, speak up. Use mantalk, the sweet and sour technique, and humor to get your point across. But get your point across.

Donna, a 36-year-old kindergarten teacher, was confused about what was going on between her and Greg, a man she'd been dating two months. They seemed to be getting along fine and Donna thought they had a real future together, but then Greg began calling at the last minute and forgetting to introduce her to friends he ran into when they were out. Donna knew these were little things and that Greg really did care about her but they were beginning to bother her. Since Donna had made a point of seeing that Greg made an emotional investment in the relationship, she was less reluctant than she had been in the past to bring up these minor annoyances. Donna and I designed two scripts, one a straightforward approach using the sweet and sour technique, the other a script using humor.

Sweet and Sour Script

Donna: Hello

Greg: Hello sweetheart, how are you doing?

Donna: I'm doing fine except for one thing that is really beginning to bother me. I want to talk to you about it now and clear the air.

Greg: What is it?

Donna: Well, when we first started dating, you always called ahead to make plans for us to go out. Now that we've been going out a while, you don't. I prefer it when you call ahead because it gives me an opportunity to plan my week and it makes me feel more romantic because (sweet and sour) I look forward to when I'll be seeing you again.

Greg: Oh, I didn't know it was that important to you. I'll make a point of calling ahead.

Humorous Script

This was the script Donna actually followed.

Donna: Hello.

Greg: Hello sweetheart, how are you?

Donna: Fine.

Greg: Would you like to come over tonight and watch a video and have dinner?

Donna: With everything on it or should I leave off the hot pepper and garlic?

Greg: What are you talking about?

Donna: Well, since you think of me as a pizza to be delivered right to your door at any time day or night, I just want to make sure you get exactly what you want. With or without extra cheese?

Greg: (laughing): Okay, okay, I get the message.

Donna: I'll be over in half an hour with your order.

To make her point, Donna picked up a pizza with everything on it. When he opened the door, she said, "Sir, your order has arrived."

The pizza conversation became a private joke that served to diffuse the anger between them while helping Donna get her point across whenever Greg tried to order her around. As soon as Donna sensed that Greg was being inconsiderate, she would say something like, "Would you like pepperoni or sausage on your pizza, sir?" or "With everything on it, sir?"

Greg would catch himself, laugh, and back off. Sometimes he would answer her questions and demand that the pizza be delivered immediately and Donna would reply in a weak voice, "Yes sir, as soon as possible, sir, will there be anything else, sir?" By exaggerating their roles and using humor, Donna confronted Greg with his bossiness without making him feel defensive. In the process, they developed their own way of dealing with their differences that got results for them, while still allowing Greg to "play act" his controlling behavior in a way that wasn't detrimental to the relationship.

Donna needed to make alternative plans for the week if she used the sweet and sour plan so that if he had failed to call, she wouldn't be tempted to go out with him at the last minute. If Greg had still failed to show more consideration, Donna would have had to decide how willing she was to be involved with a man whose actions said he was ambivalent about his relationship with her.

To deal with the situation where Greg failed to introduce Donna to his friends, Donna had the following (sweet and sour) statement ready. "I would appreciate it if you'd remember to introduce me to your friends when you run into them. Don't worry, I promise not to run off with one of the men, I only have eyes for you."

BREAKING BAD HABITS

It's never too late to change your own bad relationship habits. As long as you're aware of your actions, you can prevent a repeat of former behavior that served only to sabotage relationships.

Linda, a 34-year-old writer, promised herself that she would handle her relationship with Steve differently from others in the past. Even though she was taken by him and knew he could satisfy her non-negotiable needs, Linda refrained from pressing for the next step, an exclusive monogamous relationship. She resisted the urge to say "I love you" the moment she felt it, but waited a bit to measure the depth of Steve's interest in her. She began acting with forethought and determination. In addition, each day Linda asked herself at least ten times: Does he deserve me? Here are some bad habits Linda eliminated.

I used to come into work Monday morning and tell all my co-workers the details of my Saturday night, full of enthusiasm and hope for the future of my new relationships. When things fell through, as they usually did, I had to explain the disappearance of each man from my life. When I quit the Monday morning commentary on my love life, I began feeling better about not being everyone's form of soap opera entertainment.

In the past, I'd been too eager to show men off to my friends to get their approval. I'd even let my parents get into the act. This time I held off until we were beyond the initial dating stages. In fact, I met his friends before he met mine. This served to keep the romance low key and limited the expectations of those around me. It wasn't easy at first, nor did it seem natural to make a conscious effort to act in my own behalf, but it began paying off so I kept it up.

In the past I acted on emotion rather than fact and often regretted it. I held back my initial reaction of jealousy and anger after meeting Steve's ex-girlfriend at a party. What was she doing there?! However, rather than acting upset and asking for reassurance—my natural response—I forced myself to view the situation objectively. Why did his friends invite her, knowing I'd be there? If they'd hoped for a reconciliation, was it likely to occur, given how they reacted to each other? The answer was clearly no—he ignored her most of the evening. I realized she wasn't a threat and began to feel more confident about our relationship. Rather than jump to conclusions about the way Steve felt about me, I gathered facts.

Another major difference was her outlook on the relationship. In addition to the affirmations Linda said every day, she made an effort to quit being as concerned about the impressions she was making on Steve and became more concerned with the impressions *he* was making on *her*. As a result, she ended up feeling more confident and coming across that way too.

LOVESICKNESS

Once you've become involved with someone, it's easy to begin feeling lovesick and acting in ways that are not in your best interests romantically. Examine the following symptoms of lovesickness. Do you let this sort of behavior sabotage the relationship?

- Call him all hours of the day and night. You can't stop, even though you know you should.

- Drive by his place late at night to see if his car is there, or otherwise check up on his whereabouts.

- Send silly, romantic cards or long involved letters all about your "feelings." It is fine to send a card occasionally if you're sure the feeling is mutual. If you send cards too often, it makes you look desperate.

- Ask for reassurance constantly. This makes you appear insecure and unattractive. Don't expect your relationship to give you all the satisfaction you need in life. Seek other areas of interest rather than locating all your feelings of self-worth in a relationship.

Other self-destructive symptoms include eating too much, shopping too much, or talking too much about him to your friends.

Prescription for Lovesickness

Don't feel depressed if you've been acting lovesick. It's not too late to backpedal. Here are some positive antidotes. They will allow you to return to acting in your own best interests.

Be a moving target. If you are waiting around for a man to phone you, Remember—men are much more attracted to a moving living target. Keep busy.

Buy an answering machine. You must get an answering machine. Let him leave a message if you're busy. You can get back to him. When you go out, avoid the temptation to call in for your messages every fifteen minutes. If you are home when he calls, don't pick up on the first ring and immediately invite him over.

Avoid phone sex. Don't encourage long phone conversations, especially if they take place late at night and seem to be replacing regular get-togethers. Let him get in the habit of *seeing* you often, as opposed to being your phone buddy. Especially look out for men who find time only to call.

Don't hint for him to ask you out. If you want to ask him out, take the initiative and do so. However, if you've asked him out twice and he's refused, back off and let him make the next move.

Don't whine about not seeing enough of him. That will only make him want to run away! Instead, make him look forward to seeing you by not always being available when he wants you.

Don't call him without something to say. Mention what you enjoyed most about your last date or relate a funny story or news item he would appreciate. Have something more to say than just hello.

Stay in circulation. In order to choose the right man, you need to do some comparison shopping. Eventually you both will want to make a monogamous commitment, but now is not that time. Most women feel guilty about seeing more than one man at a time, especially if they are beginning to like him very much. And a man will often pressure a woman to date him exclusively. Do not give in to this urge or this pressure until the relationship is firmly established and the future prospects fairly secure. Men are usually territorial. For many of them it's not enough to care about a woman to want to commit to her. He must also fear losing her. How can this happen when you're not even dating other people?

Here are other reasons why dropping out of circulation is a mistake:

- It's risky. You need to diversify rather than over-invest your emotions with one man. If things don't work out, you could suffer a huge loss.

- It's not time-efficient. People in sales don't follow up one lead at a time, they work on several, realizing they won't make every sale. Don't date men one at a time. It takes too long to see how things turn out. Date several, hedge your bets, and avoid losses.

- It causes you to lose perspective. When you are seeing only one man, you are more likely to over-romanticize the relationship. Don't fall into the trap of dropping everything in your life when a worthwhile man comes along. Keep your options open.

- It causes you to appear less attractive. We all desire things that are not easy to obtain. It's human nature. To resist this truth is self-defeating. You would never tell a prospective employer that no other company was interested in hiring you. If you interviewed at a company you liked, you would never cancel interviews with other companies. It's a common practice for people to try and appear attractive and professionally desirable when seeking employment. Why should it be any different in a relationship?

Although you have gone out with a man you like very much and you believe he likes you just as much, don't be rushed into choosing him over another just because he complains the most. Plenty of men take their time to narrow the field. A woman should not feel guilty or inconsiderate when she does the same.

Resist urges to make long-range plans with him, to spend your vacation together, or even to spend holidays with each other. Wait until you are *sure* the relationship has a future. Otherwise he'll feel you are pressuring him. Later on it will be important to do these things together, but not yet.

Don't become a Stepford Wife. Don't try to mold yourself into some man's perfect ideal. Forget about trying to be his fantasy woman. Just be yourself. Of course you try to make a good impression, but don't go overboard.

Patricia, a 37-year-old nursing supervisor, took up all the sports that Darrell, her new boyfriend, enjoyed. Although she'd never really been that athletic before, Patricia took up skiing, tennis, running, and sailing. She spent a fortune on lessons, equipment, and clothing. Finally after eight months of sprains, aches, and pains, she told Darrell she'd prefer going someplace warm where she could shop, rather than a weekend of skiing. Darrell was shocked. He accused Patricia of faking all his interests in order to make him fall in love with her. Fate helped Patricia out because Darrell had a knee injury that prevented him from participating in a lot of the sports he enjoyed. Suddenly they became "compatible" again and Darrell forgave her.

Although we all tend to overaccommodate in the early stages of a relationship, don't become someone you're not. It may work well in the short term, but overaccommodation will lead to resentment and the person you had hoped to win will feel the victim of false advertising.

You can spend virtually all of your time together if you both have similar interests. That's why it's sometimes tempting to pretend you do. Of course you may genuinely pick up new interests from men in your life, but don't change your lifestyle and interests according to your date's preferences. Ask yourself whether you really like the activities or whether you are pretending. Have you actually been enriched by your differences and truly adopted some of his interests? Remember to be yourself. You don't have to share everything in order to be compatible.

ADVANCED TRIGGERS FOR THE LATER STAGES OF DATING

Like the memory triggers that you used initially to remind a man to call you for a date, advanced memory triggers have long-term impact on a man and need to be reinforced frequently. The advanced trigger associates you in his mind with a particular stimulus any time he sees, hears, tastes, or smells it. Once you have invaded all his senses, he'll never be able to get you out of his mind.

Perfume. Perfume manufacturers understand the lasting impact of smell, which is why they spend millions researching new scents. Without spending too much, experiment with a few perfumes until he lets you know you're wearing his favorite. After that, wear the scent always. Leave it trailing behind you at his place. He'll be constantly reminded of you.

Music. When you're in his car listening to the radio, notice what kind of music he prefers. Designate a theme song for your relationship, play it on special occasions to trigger his memory of the early, most exciting days of your courtship.

Food. If you enjoy cooking, learn what his favorite dish is and serve it when you want him in a very receptive mood. If you don't like to cook, discover a favorite restaurant and rendezvous there romantically. Reserve these treats of his favorite home-cooked meal or dinner out for occasional use, to remind him of the good times.

Ginny, a 38-year-old ballet instructor, decided she wanted to try using a food trigger to arouse her boyfriend's hunger for her. Ginny began seductively feeding William a chocolate-dipped strawberry right before she anticipated they were going to make love. Later on in their courtship, when they had both gotten distracted and seemed to be drifting away, Ginny would buy chocolate-covered strawberries and feed them to William. It reminded them of how sensual their relationship could be and got them back into the mood to see for themselves.

Visuals. Find out what he loves to see you wear. Neal thinks I look best in hats. He loves to see me in them and so occasionally I do wear them. I make a point of wearing hats during the most pleasant time of the year for us, our vacation. When I'm at home and wear the same type of hat I did on vacation, it reminds us both of the relaxing time we had and how much we enjoyed ourselves. Other visual triggers can be a framed photograph of the two of you, or personalized license plates—use his nickname and he'll think of you whenever he gets in the car.

Self Triggers

It's easy to falter and return to old, destructive ways of relating to men that damage your self-esteem. Avoid wasting time this way by using self-triggers that reinforce your commitment to acting in your own best interest.

A support person. Have someone who understands your quest

to find a mate and supports you in trying new approaches and behaviors. Maybe you and a woman friend who's read this book and is also ready to start taking control of her love life can compare notes and keep each other motivated.

Stickers. I have my clients place stickers I designed for them in various places they are bound to see them throughout the day. One sticker, which is popular for putting in compacts, says "Don't tell him, tell your therapist." Under this text there is space for your therapist's number in case you need an emergency consultation. Another sticker, to go in a diaphragm case, says, "Have you bonded with him yet?" One used for the mirror reads, "Act the way you want to feel." You can design stickers to reinforce any Romance Management principles by picking up adhesive name tag-badges at a stationery store and placing them, with your personal trigger, anywhere you know you'll be seeing them throughout the day.

WHERE DO YOU STAND?

One of the reasons women often feel vulnerable about their relationships is because they don't always know just where they stand with a man they've been dating. There is a certain amount of uncertainty inherent in dating, but after you've been going out for a while, especially if you've been sleeping together, you want to know the score. Ask yourself the following questions about his behavior.

Do you date on the weekend? If he does not work on weekends, yet has never asked you out on the weekend, he's probably dating others. He may even have a "steady" girlfriend he sees regularly. Until you've been dating on the weekend, it's not wise to assume he's very available for a relationship. Proceed with caution and keep your options open.

How often does he ask you out? Consider the frequency of your dates when measuring a man's interest in you. If you go out consistently once or twice a week—once during the week and once on the weekend, for instance—you are establishing a dating pattern that is comfortable, predictable, and conducive to establishing a stable, long-term relationship. If, on the other hand, he dates you infrequently, even if it is on the weekend, you may still have a future together, but not at the moment. Avoid focusing all your time and energy on winning over this elusive type. See him if you like, but not at the last minute and not to the exclusion of all others.

Have you gotten to the point when you spend the holidays together? If you've been dating a few months or more, and consider your relationship a serious one, you should be spending your holidays and other special occasions such as your birthdays together. Beware of a man who doesn't spend family holidays with you because he is reluctant to introduce you to his family. Don't push it at first, but after a year of steady involvement, you should be concerned.

Does he call regularly to share the events of his week and see how you're doing? This is an excellent sign that you are on his mind. Don't always be the one to call. If you do, he won't be able to establish the good habit of calling *you* regularly.

DANGEROUS SITUATIONS

The man you're involved with shows little consideration for your needs and the situation is getting worse. You need to establish ground rules with him and backpedal to get results. Refer back to Chapter Two and review how to do this.

The bad clearly outweighs the good, but you cling to old memories of the past and hope things will improve. Don't live in a fantasy world. All relationships have an ebb and flow, but if things don't get better, you'll have to quit living in the past and move on. You have nothing to lose by taking action. Use mantalk to let him know what you want in the relationship. Write a script in short concise mantalk statements to use with your man to get your point across. Follow your words up with actions. If things don't improve, cut your losses and move on.

You think the man you're dating is your ideal mate, but there is another woman in the wings and he isn't willing to date you exclusively. Don't forget one of the most basic romance rules—

date only men who are available. A man who is seriously involved with another woman is not available. It's hard to know at first whether there is another contender among the women he knows, but if there is, move on. Don't enter a competition to win him.

You must make endless compromises in order to keep the relationship together. If you begin doing all the emotional work in the relationship and making all the compromises, he is liable to become more detached because he no longer has to invest emotionally in the relationship. Make sure he works on negotiation and compromise issues with you. If he's not willing to make an investment, he's not worth your investing in him.

Every woman in the later stages of dating should be able to make the following statements.

- I don't allow myself to feel guilty about dating more than one man because I realize it is important to do comparison shopping. When the time comes to focus on one man exclusively, he will also wish to focus exclusively on me.

- I have begun establishing personal relationship triggers.

- I understand the concept of IPR and how powerful it can be in maintaining a man's interest in a relationship.

- I keep my dating diary updated at every stage of my relationship.

- I decide how much time to spend with men, and I have sex only when we *both* wish to.

- I understand lovesickness often occurs in the early stages of a romance. Rather than sabotage my romance, I will employ antidotes which will assist me in maintaining my self-esteem.

ROMANCE RULE #6:

In order to choose the right man you need to do some comparison shopping.

ROMANCE RULE #7:

Romance Management is important at every stage of your courtship.

COMMIT OR QUIT

Even if you're on the right track, you'll get run over if you just sit there.

—WILL ROGERS

Y OU'VE identified your non-negotiable needs. You've prospected for eligible men, and have been dating more than one for some time. Congratulations! You're ready to commit or quit.

It's now time to examine the bottom line of your relationships by filling out the Final Analysis worksheet. This will determine which of your dating partners best satisfies your non-negotiable needs. Next, follow your intuition to determine if you have any chemistry with that particular man. If you do, you should begin following strategies to secure a commitment. If you have no chemistry of attraction between you, no matter how good his cost-benefit analysis looks, he's all wrong for you. If the Final Analysis sheet shows he will not meet your needs, it is also time to quit and move on. Breaking up is hard to do, but this chapter will guide you through the process. Ultimately, you will feel thankful you moved on because you will be free to enter a fulfilling relationship.

The cost-benefit analysis you perform on the worksheet titled the Final Analysis helps you review your relationship objectively. Don't guess about anything so important as your romantic future. By looking at the facts in black and white, you can clearly judge the prospects of a potential match.

Although it may sound a little bold to compare love and real estate, a friend who bought a "fixer-upper" offered me the perfect analogy for this stage of a relationship.

When I bought this place I thought it only had a leaky roof, rusty pipes, and a broken radiator. Three years and a second mortgage later, here I am still pouring money into this place in an attempt to recoup my investment. Underneath a seller's fresh coat of paint, were hidden major structural damages. I purchased the house hastily because I fell in love with its charm. Blinded, I didn't do my homework and examine the contractor's report. Now I feel like I'm reliving my last relationship only this time with a house.

In real estate the escrow period offers you ample time to do all the necessary homework to see whether the property is worth the price. It also gives you a chance to view the property several times to determine whether it was really love at first sight or just infatuation.

In relationships, dating is your escrow period. It offers you time to gather information and make a wise investment. But in love, instead of examining owner disclosure statements and contractor's reports, you listen to and observe your man. Then you analyze whether the relationship is worth the emotional investment you intend to make. If you don't do your homework, you may make a bad emotional investment. Take the time now to fill out the cost-benefit analysis sheet to determine if he is a "fixer upper" or a major and uncertain overhaul.

THE FINAL ANALYSIS

You identified your non-negotiable needs before you began prospecting. If you haven't committed them to memory, tattooed them to your thigh, or pinned them to your bra, you should review them now.

Your non-negotiable needs help you resist the urge to get distracted by someone who is wrong for you. The cost-benefit analysis compares what you want with what a man has to offer. It provides you with the balance sheet revealing the pros and cons of commitment. Decide if he satisfies enough of your non-negotiable needs. If not, avoid the temptation to rearrange your priorities just because you feel you have good chemistry. Be true to yourself. Recognize his shortcomings. Don't compromise on what you really want. Hold out and resist being distracted by a quickening heartbeat. There are men who are right for you, but you will never meet them if you keep making exceptions for the wrong men.

Sometimes a compensating factor will balance everything out. If it does, then the relationship is fair and equitable. If not, you may have sold out and will probably regret it. Begin by

THE FINAL ANALYSIS

SCREENING OBJECTIVELY FOR YOUR NON-NEGOTIABLE NEEDS

Non-Negotiable Needs:	Candidate A:	Candidate B:
1.		
2.		
3.		
4.		
5.		
6.		
7.		
8.		
9.		
10.		

Compensating factors:	Candidate A:	Candidate B:
1.		
2.		
3.		
4.		

looking over the man's personality profile. Does he satisfy your non-negotiable needs? Below is the cost-benefit analysis of two men that Mary Beth had been dating for four months. Mary Beth met Rob, candidate A, through a personals ad. She met Ted, candidate B, through a video dating service. Mary Beth had completed their personality profiles and was preparing to decide which relationship to quit, and which to move toward a commitment.

Mary Beth's Non-Negotiable Needs

He must be considerate. He will be able to give as well as receive in a relationship and not expect me to maintain a career and the house by myself. He must be a helpmate in every way.

He must be willing to accept me as a package deal with my six-year-old daughter, Elizabeth. I would expect him to be an enthusiastic stepparent.

He must be willing to have at least one more child. I understand this could rule out some men who have already had children.

He must have a sense of humor. I need to be with a man who doesn't take himself too seriously, who can make me laugh and appreciate my off-beat sense of humor and practical jokes.

Physically I prefer a man who is a little solid and in good shape. A nice broad chest is a must.

He must have the ability to communicate. No quiet and moody types. He must be willing to compromise and work things out between us rather than expect me to do all the emotional upkeep in the relationship.

He must be ready for a monogamous relationship and eventually marriage.

He must be willing to accept the fact that I will be traveling a week out of each month for work. He would be supportive of my career and agree that I should return to work after we had children.

He must be financially independent, with a stable career. He cannot be a workaholic and I prefer that he not travel on his job.

He must make me feel good about myself when I'm with him, and not be critical or overly demanding.

This is how candidates A and B stacked up on Mary Beth's cost-benefit analysis.

Y = Yes   N = No   M = Maybe

	A Rob	B Doug
1) Considerate	Y	Y
2) Package deal	Y	Y
3) More children OK	Y	Y
4) Sense of humor	M	Y
5) Not skinny	Y	Y
6) Communication skills	M	Y
7) Monogamy	M	Y
8) Agree to working-mom status	N	Y
9) Financially secure	Y	Y
10) Makes me feel good	Y	Y

Candidate A. Rob was the man Mary Beth met through her personals ad. He had strong feelings about women staying at home to raise their children. Therefore he wouldn't have been considerate regarding housework, sharing childrearing, and all the other day-to-day details of running a household.

Rob's traditional outlook amused Mary Beth at first. She found it almost charming and old-fashioned. But she wisely realized that in the long run, her life would be miserable if she had to share it with a man who would be fighting her choices every step of the way. How could they possibly communicate and get along in other areas of their lives if they were always in conflict over basic issues?

Rob's compensating factors, the fact that he wanted to have children and physically appealed to her, didn't outweigh all the negatives. Mary Beth moved on rather than hanging on and trying to change Rob's outlook or compromise her own. She simply told Rob she liked him a lot, but they were too different to be together. Mary Beth didn't allow Rob to sweet talk her into changing her mind. She realized their basic outlooks were too opposed and that she wouldn't ever be able to change his basic philosophy about life and what role women should play in it. Though it was painful, Mary Beth moved on.

Candidate B. Doug satisfied all of Mary Beth's non-negotiable needs according to the cost-benefit analysis. Doug and Mary Beth shared many of the same interests and there was strong physical attraction between them. Mary Beth knew she was on the right track romantically when she decided to quit dating Rob and concentrate on moving her courtship forward with Doug.

CHEMISTRY

You must have strong positive chemistry with a man before you can commit to a future together. Because this is a matter of heart, rather than head, it has received less attention in this book. Chemistry IS a thing which just happens. And it is essential to a relationship. When you don't click with a man, it is like not clicking with a job. Your instincts tell you it just isn't working. Most of us know people who have been forced into work that didn't make use of their natural abilities, and in fact called upon abilities they didn't possess (such as arithmetic for a math phobic).

The same applies to relationships with men. If you seem to have no chemistry with a man, you'll have little effect on him. A long-term involvement with a man who doesn't return your affections will erode even the strongest self-respect. You want to be with a man who will remind you daily of how wonderful you are, not how inadequate! Even if his cost-benefit analysis is excellent, no secret love potion or black magic will win him over if he is neutral about you. Romance has to build on something stronger than indifference. When a man doesn't feel any chemistry for you, you must walk away from him, as painful as it will be, so that you can search for a relationship that will enhance your self-esteem rather than detract from it.

Women whose fathers were distant or difficult to please are often attracted to indifferent men. They replay with the men in their lives the role they played with their fathers. If this sounds like you, or if you have low self-esteem and continue seeking out men who agree with your low assessment of yourself, look into short-term therapy.

Avoid falling into the trap of justifying a man's behavior if you know he's lukewarm rather than wild about you. Even if simply being with him is enough for you now, a one-sided love will make you miserable. To remind yourself of this, tune into country stations and listen to the scores of songs that have been written pain and suffering as a result of unrequited love. Even if you don't like country music, listen anyway so you can get a feel for what's in store for you if you stay in the wrong relationship.

YOUR TIME FRAME

Once you draw near the second-year mark, you are leaving behind the honeymoon phase of your relationship. He may begin losing the incentive to marry as the infatuation and passion begin to cool off a bit.

Refer back to the time frame you set for yourself in Chapter Two. You may want to revise it, but at least it keeps you focused on a goal. If you haven't already done so, write the day you wish to marry in a place you'll see daily, such as on your desk calendar or daily planner. When you set your long- and short-term goals for the year, don't forget to include your romance goals as well.

In securing a commitment, timing is a delicate issue. You know, from having taken his personality profile, what time-related issues he has in mind with regard to his career and education. During the commit-or-quit phase you must analyze his emotional readiness as well. In this area your intuition comes into play. Honestly assess how interested he is in you and the relationship.

Length of Involvement

You need to have been dating steadily and monogamously for at least six months before you begin talking about a marriage commitment. Ideally, you should become engaged a year and a half after you meet him and marry before your second year together. Otherwise his interest will have peaked and now be dying down. Best to strike when he's most receptive—between the twelfth and eighteenth month of your courtship.

Extenuating Circumstances

What if he says he has other obligations now and wants to wait until some time in the future to marry? This could be tricky.

Did he mention these obligations earlier or did they come out of the blue? Were you aware of the fact that he wanted to return to law school or did he just suddenly tell you he's decided to write a novel that requires him to go into total seclusion? When he says "sometime in the future," he's being vague. You'll need to know what it means. Be direct. Ask him how long does he think it will be before he's ready to get married? Then you'll need to compare his estimated time frame with yours. An ideal courtship proceeds through the initial dating, or fascination, phase, when your attraction is primarily chemical. It lasts from the day you meet until it dawns on you that he's got flaws. Between three to six months should move you into a monogamous relationship. Involvement with a man who sees others may be both emotionally and physically draining. Set limits on the amount of time you'll wait.

How long is reasonable to wait depends on your time frame. Two years from the time you meet a man until you marry is generous. If he is younger than you, he may be reluctant. Men don't face the childbearing biological clock. They can father children until old age, so they aren't as motivated to marry as women are. Since they have their own agendas, they can feel pressured and resentful about satisfying a woman's agenda rather than their own. You must take into consideration his personal time frame when approaching the commit-or-quit phase of your romance. But if his time to marry is too far off from your own, you must quit the relationship.

Commit or Quit Danger Signals

There are other women. You've been dating over a year and he's still not ready for a monogamous relationship. He expects you to wait. Don't allow a man to make you feel desperate or insecure for wanting to get a commitment, and don't spend too much time waiting around for him to decide. Create the mindset that allows you to trust your instincts and concentrate on fulfilling your dreams. This means you have faith that if you leave the wrong relationship you will find the right one. When you act out of strength and a belief in yourself, you draw men to you. Give him a deadline for monogamy. If he doesn't give the others up, you give him up. Never stay around to compete for him.

You fight all the time. For some couples, constant sniping is a form of entertainment. The tension and uncertainty infuses a little passion in their lives. This is fine if you both unconsciously realize it as such. But if your friends no longer want to discuss your relationship with you and you're embarrassed to tell your family that you're still together, your fighting is getting out of hand.

If you fight all the time and about trivial topics, you may be skirting the real issue of your anger. Moreover, if you're having problems now, your differences will be magnified after you marry. If you love each other and believe the relationship has potential, you might consider premarital counseling to help you uncover your differences and learn how to negotiate and compromise with each other.

HOW TO END A RELATIONSHIP THAT'S ALL WRONG FOR YOU

There's a certain excitement involved in not knowing whether a relationship will work out. But if you want to take control of your love life, you'll have to give up that dubious pleasure for something better. Don't let your relationships drag on until they end like a last scene of tragic drama. End the relationship now.

How to Quit

- Be polite, but firm. Don't lead a man on and let him think you mean maybe when you really mean no.

- Be straightforward. Tell him face to face. Don't prolong the agony for him. That will make you feel guilty about breaking it off.

- Don't slide back into the relationship because you're too lazy to look for someone else. If you have not been dating other men, make a commitment to do a market search for new men as soon as you've regrouped from ending your relationship.

- Don't try to be "just friends" with him, at least not for a while. This rarely works out. It's not fair to allow him to hope you'll change your mind if you know you wouldn't. It's especially cruel if he loves your kids. Make a clean break rather than offering him unrealistic hope.

- Don't keep him on as a maintenance man, still sleeping with you and dating until you find someone better. You need to be uninvolved to recognize and be available for all the possibilities.

Sometimes you have to break up with a man you love, but who is all wrong for you. When you know your relationship is doomed, you need to end it now rather than drawing out the pain and frustration. This is in your best interest, and actually it is also in his best interest.

- Quit putting it off. Decide on a date to end your relationship and write it right here_____.

- Plan to have a period of mourning for your relationship during which you can take off work and recover from the lovesickness and withdrawal of your lost love.

- Call a friend who knows of your circumstances and arrange to stay with her for a few days to keep from feeling so lonely that you call him up and invite him over. If during the first two weeks of your breakup you have a strong urge to go back, continue to stay with a friend, take a brief vacation, or to visit relatives.

- Make plans to spend time doing things with friends, develop a new hobby, or enroll in a class in order to distract yourself.

Pressure to Maintain a Relationship

It may seem cold-hearted to end a relationship just because a man can't satisfy your non-negotiable needs. But if he can't, he won't make an appropriate mate for you. Some women feel sorry for the man they're dating and don't want to disappoint him. Other people can also lead a woman to believe she is lucky to have any relationship at all, so she remains in one that is unacceptable. If that describes you, monitor your exposure to such people.

- *Your family.* If your family is constantly asking you who you're dating and when you're getting married, you will feel pressured. Tell them if they're in such a hurry to see you married, they can pay a matchmaker or your membership in a video dating service. You'd be surprised to know how many memberships are purchased this way. Have the company you prefer put your parents on their mailing list.

- *Your friends.* Your friends are all getting married and you feel like you're being left out. Don't be tempted to rush into anything just because your friends are picking out their china patterns. Take your time and choose wisely. The good news is that plenty of married couples love to play matchmaker. Go ahead and let them know what you're looking for.

- *Books and magazine articles.* Some women's magazines may lead you to believe that your expectations are too high and that there is a scarcity of available men. They urge you to settle for whoever will take you. Forget about the doomsdaying. Don't allow yourself to be brainwashed! You can and will have the relationship you deserve if you believe it can happen.

- *Friends who have already given up.* It can be very discouraging if everyone around you has already given up finding a relationship. They may attempt to halt your search for the perfect mate. You may need to distance yourself from them temporarily and make friends with women who can be more supportive of your romantic goals.

OBSTACLE TO THE ALTAR: THE LEASE-OPTION APPROACH TO LOVE

When you lease a piece of property for a set amount of time, with an option to purchase, you get what you want without

having to make a long-term commitment. The same goes for living
with someone. Don't settle for a lease-option live-in situation if
what you want is marriage.

Going on Probation

Living together will not ease a man into marriage. If he is
ambivalent, and you move in, hoping to convince him, you'll be
putting yourself on probation and the relationship on trial. The
weakest position you can take is that of trying to convince an
ambivalent boyfriend that you'd make the perfect wife. Why
should he marry you as long as you are willing to move in and
audition for the role without any promise of ever playing the
part? If you want to marry, stay focused on your goal. Studies
show that couples who live together have a higher rate of infidelity
than married couples, less satisfaction with their ability to communicate, and more likelihood of divorce after marriage than
couples who don't cohabit before marriage. Why? The most popular theory is that couples who live together are less committed
to their relationships than couples who marry. If you must move
in with a man, do so intelligently. Use common sense and take
certain actions so you won't be emotionally and financially devastated if things don't work out.

If your goal is marriage, don't move in on a trial basis
without a wedding date. Wait until he's agreed to marry and set
a date a year from when you agree to live together. Have him
move in with you. If you must move in with him, maintain your
apartment so you feel less like his tenant and so you have a
place to live if things go bad. Don't quit your job and become
his housekeeper. Never buy property together until after you
marry.

Some women say they're uncertain about whether or not to
marry a man, so they want to try a trial live-in period to help
them decide. If you are ambivalent about marrying a man, you
will not benefit from moving in with him. You are more likely
to settle with him out of convenience once you move in rather
than force yourself to go through the changes necessary to move
out and start over with someone new. Living with a man, even
if you are now dating him exclusively, limits your options and
your opportunities for meeting and dating other men.

MOVING TOWARD A COMMITMENT

Positive signs that you are moving toward a commitment include the following.

- You are seeing each other consistently, at least twice a week and maybe every night. He may have a lot of things at your place and vice versa. At this point some couples have exchanged keys.

- You've met his family and spent the holidays with them if they live nearby. You also know most of his friends and have met some people he works with.

- People think of you as a couple. Some of your friends have even asked when you're getting married.

- You've taken at least one vacation and spent at least a week together without wishing you were at home alone.

- You feel comfortable spending quiet time together, not talking but just relaxing and listening to music, reading, or watching TV. You no longer feel like you're on a date, you feel like you're in a relationship.

- You share many similar attitudes and values. You've discussed the possibility of marriage without his running away or becoming distant.

- You've discussed whether to have children. If either of you have children, you've met them by now.

His Commitment Comfort Zone

Many women complain about men who, after becoming emotionally and physically involved in a relationship, suddenly rebel and exert their independence.

Emotional hide and seek results from a man's early childhood and his need to separate from his mother so he can model himself on his father. Men are most comfortable when they can both maintain some distance and some closeness in a relationship. This need to separate and stand alone is central to a man's masculinity, but it conflicts directly with his need to be loved, nurtured, and cared for. Many men seek to satisfy both closeness and autonomy by first seeking and then hiding emotionally.

After a man has been very intimate with a woman for a prolonged period of time, he may seek to regain his emotional equilibrium by backing off. Hide and seek ensues. He seeks the intense intimacy he desires, yet avoids the commitment it entails. A man's commitment comfort zone (CCZ), the place where he is most likely to want to make a commitment to a woman, is somewhere between intimacy and independence. A woman's commitment comfort zone, on the other hand, is usually at intimacy. The smart woman learns to manipulate her man's comfort zone to align it more closely with hers. This can be tricky, but through anticipation, and awareness of the differences, and a plan of action, it is possible.

A man's commitment comfort zone becomes threatened by too much continual closeness. You shouldn't take it personally if he distances from you. He's not necessarily rejecting you, he's just feeling his commitment comfort zone being threatened. When a man's CCZ is threatened, he plays emotional hide and seek with you because of his uncertain feelings. When this occurs, you must be understanding of his comfort zone, but you must also avoid being exposed to prolonged uncertainty. Otherwise, you'll find yourself on the receiving end of a high dosage of inconsistent positive reinforcement. Under a steady diet of emotional hide and seek, you may begin to believe that your longing for love is love itself and never feel comfortable in a healthy and satisfying relationship.

The IPR schedule offers a built-in equalizer to a man's fear of commitment and backing-off behavior. It limits the consistency of exposure and intensity, thereby allowing him mini doses of distancing, which acts as an antidote to and takes the edge off his desire to escape.

All you need to do is to maintain a healthy involvement with life and self-growth outside of your primary relationship. Not spending all your free time together allows you sufficient distance to re-energize yourselves and bring something to the relationship to keep it stimulating and passionate and thriving. When you are your own person, separate from your relationship with him, you're not dependent on him for all of your emotional or social needs and he will be less frightened of commitment with you.

Men also fear that when they marry, everything in the relationship will change and they will lose control of their life and their autonomy. They fear the responsibility of having a family and the loss of options. When you acknowledge a man's fears without constantly monitoring his moods and actions, his doubts and concerns about marriage will begin to soften a bit. If he sees you have a life of your own, he may become more confident. If he seems to require separation occasionally, respect his need for a little space and don't overreact to it.

If a man you've been dating drops out of your life completely, and doesn't call or return your calls, you need to resist the temptation to beg, bribe, or seduce him back into your life. Never make it easy for a man to re-enter your life. Unless he realizes you find this behavior unacceptable, he'll repeat it. If you are eager to take him back and have a difficult time staying angry, ask yourself why. You have a right to be angry, so don't be afraid to express your feelings. To be most effective in getting your point across, your actions will speak louder than your words. When and if he works to earn back your affections, he'll value and respect the relationship more.

What do you say when you want to say yes, but you are still angry and hurt?

- Tell him you'll have to think about it. Don't return his calls or letters for two weeks. You really should be thinking about it. Are you sure you want to take him back? In the meantime, there's no reason not to date if you've met someone you like. And it's all the better if he finds out about it.

- When you finally do see him, tell him you're not sure you're ready to go back to the way things were. Meet him for lunch rather than dinner and don't ask him back to your place. If he buys you a present, thank him but tell him you really don't think you should keep it since you're not sure you'll be getting back together.

- Ask him to explain to you why things will be different in the future. If he is able to convince you he won't run away again, you may slowly allow him back into your life. But don't make the mistake of returning his affections wholeheartedly or of planning your wedding date. He should be on probation for a while in order to appreciate how lucky he is that you took him back. Now more than ever you need to act in your own best interest and insist that he treat you as you deserve.

Getting Him in the Marrying Mood

Begin by planting a seed in his mind about the positive benefits he would receive as a husband. If you have happily married-couple friends, now's the time to haul them out and let him see what wedded bliss can be like. Don't spend time with a couple who would give the wrong impression. Take a long vacation together. Begin spending more time together just relaxing and sharing domestic chores, such as washing clothes, shopping, and cooking. If you've been contemplating the purchase of a major appliance such as a TV or stereo, have him pore over the consumer reports with you and then come along to help you pick out the item and make the purchase. If you've been wanting a pet, let him help you pick it out and name it. He can help you paint your home, build shelves, do gardening, mow your lawn, or share the responsibilities of entertaining another couple at your place.

Let him know how much you could enhance his lifestyle and contribute to the relationship as a helpmate. Advertise the talents and abilities you possess that would enhance his standard of living. Let him know that you intend to contribute to your relationship as an equal and that your unique talents will be an asset to the relationship. You don't need to be a rocket scientist or a Nobel Prize winner to impress a man. Draw on your innate abilities and don't overlook your career and social skills.

If you are in real estate, offer him a free appraisal of his home or inform him of the tax benefits of owning if he rents. Educate him about property in his area and let him know that as a couple you'd take an active part in managing and investing your money. However, never agree to invest in real estate prior to marriage. Never enter into a contract with a man in order to bind him to you. It will have the opposite effect.

Offer him advice and counsel in whatever your area of specialty may be. Play the social secretary and encourage him to entertain clients more, or design a fitness and diet program that will improve his health outlook and appreciation of you. If you can convince him to try something new that will make him feel better about himself, you'll establish a real bond with him that will be hard to break. Athletic pursuits are especially effective if you enjoy them together because he will associate the good feelings with your company and forever recall your positive influence on him. This subtle approach to selling yourself is very effective. Seeing what a positive effect you've already had on his life will lessen his fear of marriage.

Next, find out what scares him most about marriage and try to resolve his fears. Often a few hints or a gentle nudge may be what it takes for some men to commit. Others need harder artillery. If your man is clearly resistant to changing the relationship and you feel in limbo, you have a few options.

You can wait it out and hope for the best. You can walk out on him now and start dating others or, you can offer an ultimatum. It's a good sign if he seems willing to talk about his fear of commitment and wants to work through it. If he says he's not ready and needs more time, wait, but not so long that you lose your self-esteem. When you no longer feel good about yourself or the relationship, you've waited long enough.

His Fears

What is your man afraid of? What concerns make him suspect marriage and commitment? Often they are very legitimate concerns.

- His parents were divorced and miserable. Who's to say it won't be the same with you? All he knows about marriage is what he grew up with. If he's already been divorced, he's especially doubtful. Let him know you understand his concerns and don't argue with him about how he should feel. He has a right to his feelings and concerns. You can't *make* him commit to you, he has to *want* to commit.

- Monogamy. He's not sure he can be faithful to just one woman. If he's voiced this concern, don't ignore it. One thing men sacrifice when they marry is the endless variety of women they have an opportunity to be with. Even if he never acts on his impulses and sees only you, he feels reluctant to give up the option. In contrast, women rarely feel they are sacrificing much by giving up sexual opportunities because monogamy is usually one of their non-negotiable needs, whether they are single or married. How do you deal with his dread of lost opportunity? Acknowledge it, accept it, and don't get defensive or take it personally, because it has nothing to do with you or the size of your thighs. Men fantasize about sexual variety no matter whom they're with. The issue is whether they act on their desire for variety. Eventually he will have to choose between you and satisfying his fantasy of having a harem of women. Don't allow him an easy way out by becoming a bitch or nag about it. Be straightforward and matter-of-fact about what your needs are and plan to move on if he can't satisfy them.

- Are you the right woman? He may truly love you, but if he hasn't had much opportunity to date because he's young, or if he just likes a lot of variety, you'll have to decide if you think he is likely to marry you.

Common Sense Advice about Commitment

- Don't take it personally if his kids don't seem to like you. They probably don't want to share him with you and maybe they feel disloyal to their mother if they befriend you. Don't try to discipline or correct them or play mommy. They do have some influence on him and if they truly dislike you, you have something to worry about.

- Avoid all-night discussions about the future of your relationship. Men hate them and they rarely get you anywhere.

- Don't feel guilty about wanting a commitment. You have a right to feel the way you do. Don't allow a man to convince you that you're insecure, demanding, or desperate for wanting a commitment.

- Get some perspective. Sometimes a little distancing can help to give you perspective. Consider going away for the weekend alone or with a friend, just to relax and sort things out. It'll give him some space and may make him realize how much he misses you. It's important to allow a man the chance to miss you—at any stage of the relationship. Otherwise he comes to expect you to be there all the time. He forgets you have a life of your own. If you truly don't have a life of your own, now is an excellent time to begin developing one. Don't call every day to report on everything you do. If you try being on your own for short periods, you will realize you can make it if things don't work out.

- Give up the role of giver goddess. If you've been acting like a giver goddess, being eager to please and anxious to win him over with your patience, kindness, cooking, and overaccommodation, you need to change your approach. Most women who fall into the giver-goddess syndrome give consistently. Hence they fail to benefit from that most powerful tool, inconsistent positive reinforcement. As a result, the man they are involved with begins to take them for granted.

Live-in arrangements often fall into this category because the woman, not wanting to blow her chances of marriage, fails to argue about sharing housework or the quality of time spent together. The predictable result is that the man grows lazy and loses the incentive to move the courtship forward. If you can learn to quit giving so much and so predictably, you'll at least get him to notice something is changing in the relationship. He will become more alert, perhaps even concerned. If you've been living with him and playing the housekeeper, you might be better off moving out and forcing him to hire a maid.

- Let him be an active lover. When you spend all your time focusing on when he'll be ready to make a commitment, and how you can expedite the process, you act won and ready to wed. This places you in a weak position because most men love deepest when they express their love actively. Unless you give him an opportunity to play the role of romantic lover, you could be creating a one-sided affair, which is doomed. Holding back on your feelings is a kind of game, but it is one that enhances your relationship and encourages your man to participate in displays of affection that will affirm his feelings for you. Feeling love for your partner and expressing it in verbal and nonverbal ways strengthens your bond. Don't you always be the one to do all the romancing.

- Recognize his nonverbal loving actions. Women are often more verbal about their feelings than men. Since men prefer to express their feelings through actions rather than words, we need to recognize their loving behavior and appreciate their language of love. The following list of loving actions I gathered from women whose lovers weren't verbal, but expressed their love in action.

Every morning when I woke up he presented me with a glass of freshly squeezed orange juice and the morning paper—not just on the weekends, but during the week too.

When I'd had a bad day at work, he'd come over and shampoo my hair in the sink then give me a great massage.

He'd make love to me tenderly and hold me in his arms all night long.

He picked up my son from school for me when I got busy. He'd take him home, cook dinner, and keep it warm for me until I got home.

He shows off for me athletically.

He'd call me up to see how my day was going or for no reason at all, just to hear my voice.

He took care of me when I was sick and had just come home from the hospital. He picked up all my medicine and cooked and cleaned for me.

He gave me a manicure and pedicure.

He took me out a lot and generally seemed concerned with my well-being.

If you allow a man the space to express himself romantically and he does nothing, either in words or actions, you must back off to see where you stand with him. Many men will stay indefinitely in a relationship if they are getting sex and companionship, even if they don't have long-term plans for the future. That's why holding back a little is always in your best interest. It lets you see whether or not he ever intends to move forward. If not, you'll have to move on.

ISSUING AN ULTIMATUM

After you've tried everything else and you are about to give up, an ultimatum is a last-ditch effort that may get you results. For an ultimatum to succeed, however, you must really mean it. Backing down on the deadline, or pretending it doesn't exist when it comes around, will only make you feel more hopeless than ever.

Don't deliver an ultimatum out of anger, or for dramatic effect. Don't do it as a threat or to punish him for something. Have a few discussions about commitment before issuing an ultimatum. Then take your stand calmly, in sincere concern for your future with or without him. If he tells you straight out he doesn't want to make a commitment, don't try to coerce him. Ultimatums work best with men who want to commit but are a bit uncertain.

Don't wait too long to issue an ultimatum. Act while you're still feeling good about yourself. You will then behave more gracefully and with better results. Realize you're acting out of strength, not weakness. It takes courage to get your life unstuck. It's more comfortable to settle in a relationship than move on, but remember your long-term goal of finding a life mate.

Be firm, but gentle. Don't offer an ultimatum over the phone. Deliver it in person, calmly, and in a matter-of-fact way. Don't argue or defend yourself if he reacts negatively. Tell him you love him, but won't wait much longer for him to make up his mind.

Arlene, a 36-year-old nurse, and Dennis, a 42-year-old engineer, met while they were both volunteering at the SPCA. They both loved animals and between them had adopted 6 dogs, 4 cats, and a rabbit. Arlene sensed Dennis could offer her the sensitivity she felt had always been lacking in her past relationships. Dennis was attracted to Arlene's high energy and athletic good looks, and the fact that his kids loved her, but he was happy with things the way they were. After three years of dating, Arlene was ready to marry but Dennis was not. After fighting for months, Arlene finally realized that she needed to offer an ultimatum soon, while they were still on reasonably good terms and while she might be able to get results. One evening after dinner at her place, Arlene broached the subject and the conversation went like this:

Arlene: Dennis, I understand that you don't want to get married right now, but I've decided I can't wait much longer for you to make up your mind. I think I can hold out another three months, but if you don't feel ready by then, I'm going to start dating other people (mantalk).

Dennis: How can you say that?

Arlene: Dennis, there is nothing I'd rather do than spend the rest of my life with you (sweet), but I want marriage and I'm not willing to settle for less (sour). I'm sure you'll never find anyone you'd be happier with than me, but I'm not going to spend the rest of my life trying to convince you of that.

Dennis: How do I know things won't turn out the way they did with Denise (his ex-wife)?

Arlene: We can create the kind of marriage we want. And besides, I'm not Denise (mantalk).

Dennis: I really feel like you're pressuring me.

Arlene: I'm sorry you feel that way, because I love you and want you to be happy (sweet). But I want to be happy too, and for me, that means marriage. Let me know what you decide (sour).

Initially Dennis was adamant about not getting married. He'd never really sampled the singles life after his divorce because he'd met Arlene so soon and totally lost interest in dating other women. He still wasn't interested in other women but nevertheless wanted to leave his options open. As an experiment, he began testing the waters by checking out singles bars near his office after work. A friend of Arlene's saw him there at happy hour and told her about it the next day at work.

Arlene wasn't surprised about Dennis's desire to sample singles life before it was too late, but she knew he loved her and would find his life shallow and empty without her. So she didn't put him on the spot about his bar hopping. In fact, she hoped he'd get his fill of it and realize his happy hours and hangovers wouldn't be worth giving her up. She took a chance that his fear of losing her would be greater than his fear of marriage, and she was right. Three months to the day she offered her ultimatum, Dennis met Arlene for lunch and proposed. After being married for three years, Dennis says the ultimatum gave him the incentive he needed to look around and realize how miserable his life would be without Arlene.

There are positive benefits to issuing an ultimatum. It forces the issue and allows you to move on in your life—one way or the other—rather than being an emotional hostage in the wrong relationship. Men are often more emotionally involved in a relationship than they let a woman know. In such cases, a well-timed ultimatum works to secure commitment. Just because he may not be as demonstrative as you are with his feelings doesn't mean they aren't real to him.

If you issue an ultimatum, and the man flees, you've found out where he stands, loud and clear. Now you can get on with your life and find someone who doesn't want to run away when you mention the M word. After delivering a post-dated ultimatum, don't keep reminding him. You've done it, so just relax and wait.

A Post-Dated Ultimatum

When you issue an ultimatum, you usually give a specific date, such as six months, by which time the man must answer. It's not uncommon to issue an ultimatum and have the date come and go without a man being willing to follow through. If he insists he needs only a little more time and you think he has promise, allow another three-month wait. If at that time he is still thinking about it, you have to call his bluff. It's best if you can try to leave on civil terms. Let him know you have to get on with your life and that you're sorry he can no longer be a part of it. You never know, you may still hear from him.

Diane, a 34-year-old receptionist, had been dating Mannie for three years when she came to see me about securing a commitment. Diane and Mannie met at a street fair when, after passing each other, they both looked back over their shoulders. After that first gaze, they became practically inseparable. In addition to their mutual fascination, Diane got along famously with Mannie's 12-year-old son. And there were other good signs. They had already planned—a year ahead of time—to spend their vacation together, as well as the major holidays. Mannie shared his life with her. She knew all his friends and family, and they all loved each other. Everything was picture perfect except that Diane wanted to get married and Mannie didn't. Whenever Diane brought up the subject, Mannie expressed reluctance. His divorce from a childhood sweetheart had been painful and he feared a repeat performance. Why couldn't she just be happy with the way things were?

Diane was tempted to stay with Mannie on his terms. But after being a bridesmaid in her best friend's wedding, she knew she was only kidding herself. Diane wanted children and the security of a marital commitment, not a steady boyfriend. Diane was so concerned about the future of her relationship with Mannie she was constantly asking him if he still cared and whether or not he loved her. She knew it irritated him, but she couldn't help herself. She was pressing for him to be more expressive of his feelings and more affectionate too.

One thing that had attracted Mannie to Diane in the beginning of their relationship was her confidence. Now Mannie felt Diane was acting insecure and uncertain about the future of their relationship. They were spending less time having fun since almost all their time was taken up talking about their relationship. Predictably, Mannie was beginning to feel that the pain of being with Diane outweighed the pleasure. He felt she was too needy and it scared him. He missed the sexy, free-spirited woman he once knew.

Diane began by making a conscious effort not to ask compulsively for reassurance and affection from Mannie. He, in turn, began to give more freely because he felt less obligated. Diane then examined her options. She could either continue as she had, or set a time limit on how long she would wait for Mannie to make up his mind.

Diane issued an ultimatum to Mannie, calmly and lovingly, by saying she had never loved anyone more, but at the end of four months if he hadn't changed his mind about marriage, she would have to move on. They'd had many discussions about marriage and he knew where she stood on the issue. As soon as she set the date, four months from that day, she began to feel more in control of her life. She even took a look around her at some of the available men she had met since being with Mannie. She imagined what it might be like to date them. By playacting what it would be like if she were single, she discovered it wouldn't be so bad. She began to feel better about herself. Mannie noticed the difference and they began getting along better and feeling more attracted to each other again.

As her date grew closer, Diane made a point of not bringing the issue up again. Diane knew Mannie hadn't taken her seriously when she issued the ultimatum. He assumed she'd gotten it out of her system and forgotten about it, especially since they were getting along so well. But Diane hadn't forgotten. On the deadline day, Diane tearfully said good-bye. She said she loved him, but she wanted to marry so she thought they should break up and see other people.

For about two weeks Mannie was in shock. It had been so long since Diane had mentioned marriage, Mannie had hoped she'd given up on the idea. After a month Mannie began calling Diane up with weak excuses for getting to talk to her. Once he called to say he was sorry for the break-up and how much he must have hurt her. Diane told him not to apologize because she was much happier since they split and she was sorry if he didn't feel the same way. Soon, Mannie was showing up on Diane's doorstep wanting to talk.

Mannie tried to sweet-talk Diane into seeing him again, but she held firm. She began dating a man from work, though she still loved Mannie, and friends told her they'd seen Mannie out with a woman who looked almost exactly like her. It was obvious to Diane that Mannie was trying to recreate their relationship with another woman and she knew it wouldn't work.

After a three-month separation, Mannie finally came to his senses. He stopped Diane as she was coming out of her house one morning and told her that having a look-alike wasn't enough, he wanted the real thing. Diane didn't hesitate to say yes and they were married a week later. Diane is thankful Mannie had a chance to try and replace her because now he realizes how impossible it would be to do.

Here is the story of another post-dated ultimatum.

Ramona, a 38-year-old airline stewardess, was in love with David, a writer, and had been pressing for a commitment for three years.

David had a history of long-term serial monogamy. He said he was philosophically opposed to marriage and that I shouldn't take it personally. I wanted to have children, but as open-minded as I am, I just wasn't willing to have a child without marriage. We argued about it all the time. I made every possible mistake, including giving up the lease on my rent-controlled apartment, selling all my furniture, and moving into David's place to be his cook, maid, and lover. I guess I thought we were Ozzie and Harriet or something because we sure did play the roles, except we weren't married.

I was feeling desperate when I began applying Romance Management to my dying relationship. First I mastered mantalk. One of the major problems we had was that David didn't listen to anything I said. He couldn't even remember to pick up a carton of milk if I asked him to, so I finally had to start pinning notes to his coat. It was hard at first, but I began speaking in short, concise sentences to David, and telling him things directly, without so much explaining about why. This was really difficult for me because I always felt like I had to explain myself. I spoke mantalk about the housework for a week and got results. It was a great success for me because up until that point, I might as well have been speaking in tongues for all the help from him I got around the house.

One morning I simply said I was no longer going to be cleaning up for him or cooking until he began sharing some of the shopping and cleaning. Everything went along as usual that week until David's life slowly began to fall apart. His suit never got taken to the cleaners, he ran out of clean towels (I had my own stash), and all of his underwear was dirty so he had to go out and buy more. He had to wear dirty shirts and we spent a fortune eating out every night. He finally called a truce and we began working as a team. He backslid occasionally, but for the most part we never had any more major problems as soon as I quit complaining and started following my words up with actions.

After having such success using mantalk on the housekeeping issue, I had the courage to approach the marriage issue. On the fourth of July, after watching the fireworks, I said, "I love you and want to be your wife by the New Year. If you don't ask me to marry you by then, I will ask you." I felt a ton of relief after that and I know David did too because there was a renewed tranquility between us I hadn't felt in years.

With the real issue out in the open, we snapped at each other less, and I felt less uncertain, knowing things were finally drawing to a conclusion. David and I would marry or else I would move on and find another man whose timetable was more compatible with mine. As the months went by, I never brought up the subject of my ultimatum again. I became more at peace with the idea of leaving the relationship and was preparing myself for the worse by January.

But, as the New Year came closer, things began to change. David began to pick up on the fact that I was creating a new world for myself in preparation

for the possibility of our break-up. He noticed me
looking at the want ads for apartments every day and
how I seemed to be spending more time with friends.
When he mentioned the subtle change in me, I just
said I was getting ready for my walking papers and
laughed. We'd collected so many things over the
years, I knew it would take me a long time to sort
through everything, so I began packing a month
early. When David came home and saw me sorting
through all my books and knickknacks, he was pretty
shook up. He started acting more possessively after
that, telling me how much he loved me and didn't
want to lose me. He offered to start a family if I wanted
to. But my feelings hadn't changed. Calmly I told him I
was old-fashioned and would feel like I was living in a
commune rather than a home without a marriage license. After only bringing up the subject twice in five
months, it seemed like what I was saying was finally
sinking in.

I never got around to packing all my things because a few days later, we both took off work and went
down to city hall. I'd never really wanted a big wedding and David had never really wanted a wedding
before at all, so city hall was just fine. A few friends
came along and we went to brunch afterwards. If I
hadn't taken a chance on acting in my own best interest I'd probably still be a full-time live-in girlfriend,
hoping, planning, scheming, and cajoling David, without ever getting any romantic results.

I wasn't playing a game—I had no intention of
backing down on my desire for a commitment. David
knew this too, because he was finally put in a position
of imagining what it would be like to spend his life
without me. That was two years ago and we now have
a six-month-old baby. David always kids me about how
getting married was my New Year's resolution. I guess
it was, and we both agree it was the best one I've made
since then.

Men often commit out of fear of loss. For that reason, an ultimatum issued for a future time is often most effective. It allows them to anticipate the separation they are going to experience after you walk out of their lives. The post-dated ultimatum is especially effective if you are actively making other changes and improvements in your life and truly preparing yourself for the possibility of an end to the relationship. Your self-care gives you an active role. You don't sit passively waiting to see what is going to happen. Don't be surprised to see that once you disengage a little bit from the relationship and regain some autonomy, he'll react to you differently. Both of you will regain some perspective on what brought you together in the first place. Sometimes when you're too close to something, you can't see it.

What do you do when you've offered an ultimatum and are waiting for the outcome?

Designate one close friend to be your break-up buddy. Make sure it's someone who will promise to be available to you during this difficult time. Call your buddy up and keep her or him informed about what's happening. Report on what you are doing to maintain your self-esteem. Once you issue the ultimatum, try to put it out of your mind except when you talk to your break-up buddy or other close friends who know you well. If you will have to move out, or make other major adjustments in your life, don't plan to do it all at the last minute. Call on friends to help you prepare for this transition in your life. If you've been living with the man and are not working, prepare to return to the work force. Begin now to seek a job or training. Compile a list of things you've been wanting to do that you haven't had time for. On your monthly calendar plan weekly events to explore alone or with a friend. Take some time to discover what interests can bring you joy outside your relationship.

During this time of transition take exceptionally good care of yourself by eating right and exercising. Many women say they feel a real load has been lifted off their shoulders once they tell a man about their time frame. Others feel like they want to start explaining themselves and trying to talk him into it rather than just letting it sink in. Either way, plenty of exercise will help to alleviate some of your anxiety about the future.

An Immediate Ultimatum

An immediate ultimatum forces his hand now, this minute. It's either yes or no, or I'll get back to you within the next few days. Although you issued the ultimatum to feel more in control, an immediate ultimatum usually makes you feel more out of control than ever, waiting for the verdict. In addition, an immediate ultimate gives the man no time to think about what he will be losing if he loses you. Immediate ultimatums are usually issued in a moment of anger and often regretted. If you issue an ultimatum during a fight and later regret that you did, you may try to change it into a post-dated ultimatum before your man has a chance to give you an answer.

If you issue an immediate ultimatum and he doesn't even call you back, you've got to put an end to it. Call him up, say it's over, and forget him. If he comes to his senses and shows up a week, a month, or a year later and wants to change his ways, take him back on certain conditions only: that he will commit to you and the relationship.

HIS PREMARITAL ANXIETY ATTACK: WHEN HE GETS COLD FEET

Once you both agree to marry, don't be surprised if your man has a brief premarital anxiety attack. It's common for men to rebel against marriage and the women they love in order to exert their independence one last time. How successfully he recovers from his attack will have a great deal to do with the way you react to it. Premarital anxiety attacks often occur when a man suddenly wants to take a trip (escape) a few weeks before the wedding. The following two examples show how the women dealt successfully with the premarital attack.

Christine discovered that William had a frightful case of premarital anxiety when he informed her three weeks before their wedding that he intended to take a car trip around the country with his buddy, since it might be his last chance to see the States. He promised her he'd be back before their wedding and began to pack for his trip. I advised Christine to encourage William to take his trip and to share in his enthusiasm. She even neglected last-minute wedding plans to help him pack and shop for supplies he might need. Because Christine was willing to let William exert his independence, he felt less need to rebel. After four days on the road, he gave up the trip and flew home because he missed Christine and felt like a fool. Christine had been a little worried about whether or not William was going to make it back, but had she kept him from going, he might still be feeling like he wanted to escape after the wedding.

Allowing William to do as he pleased about the trip let him know that as his wife Christine didn't intend to take away all of his independence. She passed a test that William may not have even known he was giving her. Though Christine's approach was successful, she never brought up with him the subject of his anxiety attack or the fact that she used Romance Management to solve the problem. She learned from the experience that William needed to feel he wasn't being controlled, or losing out, as a result of being married.

As a form of marriage insurance, Christine does not make a fuss if William wants to take off work for a day to sail with friends or explore new interests. Christine realizes how important to William's happiness a sense of independence and adventure is. She maintains her independence as well, running her own business and constantly meeting new friends. By exploring life both together and on their own, they can each bring something back to the relationship to help it nurture and grow.

Sometimes premarital attacks can cause a real threat to the relationship. This was the case for Holly. Doug informed Holly that he had decided to crew on a boat that was leaving San Francisco and heading for Hawaii. That sounded reasonable enough, considering that he had plenty of time to get back for the wedding. However, after pressing Doug for more details, she found out everyone on the boat would be single, including the four women who were also acting as crew. Doug was a serious sailor and had never given her reason to doubt his integrity before, so she controlled her negative reactions until she could calm down and decide what the best approach would be. Holly knew that Doug was either testing her or else was planning a real escape. She had no idea what to do. She would have offered to join him but didn't know how to sail and got seasick whenever she went near water.

We decided that Holly should act confident and avoid making an issue of Doug's behavior. If he decided to go, Holly would have to trust him. As the day of the trip grew nearer, Holly kept herself busy with friends and last-minute wedding plans. When Doug mentioned the trip one night, Holly joked that she hoped he didn't fall overboard and disappear for the wedding. She loved Doug and trusted him. If he needed to take this trip to prove something, she had decided to let him go ahead. If he went and decided he didn't want to marry, it was best that she find that out now.

Two days before the trip, Doug decided not to go because he didn't think he'd have enough time to get back for the wedding. Holly knew the real reason was that he lost the desire to bolt. When Doug didn't get any resistance from Holly about his provocative behavior, his fears about losing his independence lessened and his premarital anxiety attack died down.

Unless a man's attack is prolonged, it probably isn't serious. Your best bet is to let him get it out of his system so he won't resent you later.

Some premarital attacks are more subtle. Like the common cold, they have no cure, but most strains will die out naturally if you don't make too much of a fuss. Humor always works well.

One man refused to wear a suit, tie, or socks at the wedding. His girlfriend outdid him by showing up in shorts. Another planned to meet his former girlfriend for lunch a week before the wedding and made sure his fiancée knew about it. She showed up at the same restaurant with a handsome stranger, who proceeded to strip down to a g-string while dancing around her table, then waltzed out the door with her. Needless to say, he got the point.

Commit or Quit Checklist

- I don't allow a man to make me feel unreasonable for wanting a commitment.

- I realize moving in with a man is the weakest position a woman can be in.

- I realize that when a man begins to distance himself, I need to concentrate on spending time with friends and exploring my own interests to let him know I have a life of my own separate from him.

- I understand how to react to a man's premarital anxiety attack in a way that is most conducive to matrimony.

- I have designed my commitment plan of action.

- I have decided to quit or press for a commitment on _____.

- If possible I plan to quit on ____ and vacation on ____.

Now that you understand basic Romance Management principles, you are well prepared to find a man to marry. Remember to establish the Romance Management ground rules, maintain your perspective, and know your non-negotiable needs.

It's so easy to become discouraged and fail to apply Romance Management principles. When this happens, don't be too hard on yourself. Most women find it hard to get used to acting in their own best interests. We all develop ways of reacting to situations that haven't worked but have become a habit. As you practice the principles in the book, I hope your first few successes with these techniques will be enough to motivate you to maintain their use consistently. It is what makes them so effective. Remember, you deserve a healthy relationship with a man who can satisfy your needs. Don't settle for less.

If you haven't already, decide upon your marriage date before you finish this book. Write it down in your dating diary and in several other places and so you won't lose sight of your romantic goals.

Congratulations for having the courage to take control of your love life. You now have the tools to make it happen. Good luck!

ROMANCE MANAGEMENT RULE #8:

Let him know you plan to marry and if he doesn't like the idea, use Romance Management to find a man who does.

ROMANCE & COURTSHIP

ROMANCE

R Re-evaluate your needs.

O Opportunities are out there—to meet men, take them.

M Mistakes. We all make them. Learn from them and move on.

A Adventure. Try something different. Break up the old routine. Trying new things and taking risks increases your self-esteem.

N Needs. It is not unreasonable to expect 80% of your needs to be satisfied in a relationship. You must know what they are.

C Caring about yourself is important. Do not dare someone else to care about you by not caring about yourself. Quit hiding behind extra weight or a style that does not reflect your personality.

E Effort. Finding and maintaining a romance takes effort. Expend the effort you would for any worthwhile cause and you will obtain results.

COURTSHIP

C Confidence is the key. Until you begin to feel confident, try acting as if you are. Soon your feelings will catch up to your actions.

O Optimistic. Be optimistic. Your outlook determines the reality you experience. Others react to your outlook, so make it a pleasant one.

U Understanding. It is important to understand your own finest qualities as well as your shortcomings. Be aware that a man will need to make compromises to accept you as you are and vice versa.

R Rejection. Do not allow it to keep you from taking risks. Psychologists say the one thing depressed people all have in common is that they are immobilized, afraid to take risks. Taking risks increases self-esteem. Do it!

T Tantalize. Give intermittent positive reinforcement to men, especially when you flirt. It keeps their interest. Lighten up. Be playful.

S Safe sex, smart sex. If there is any doubt in your mind about whether or not you will hear from him again, it is too soon.

H Happy. You will be happy if your life is well-balanced and harmonious. Do not focus all your interest on men and dating. You will seem desperate rather than ready. Develop your own interests and friendships.

I Improvise. Improvise in your behavior. Try different ways to react to people. Learn what works and what does not. Trying new ways of relating makes you more interesting and increases your level of confidence.

P A courtship unfolds at its own pace. Don't rush it. Relax and enjoy!

RELATIONSHIP OBJECTIVES

---

1. What is my relationship objective?

---

2. What is my time frame?

---

3. How high on my list of priorities is finding a mate?

---

4. What obstacles and roadblocks stand in my way?

---

5. What actions can I take to overcome these obstacles?

RECOGNIZING PATTERNS

EXAMINING PAST EXPERIENCES WITH MEN

(1) Do your relationships evolve slowly or do you rush into them?

_____

(2) Do you tend to draw a false early impression of men and then feel let down when the truth comes out?

_____

(3) Do you always seem to give more in a relationship than you get?

_____

(4) When you enter into relationships are you willing to accept the men as they are, or are you hoping to make major changes?

_____

(5) How long have your last three relationships lasted? Who ended it?

_____

(6) Do you like the chase but get bored because the passion never lasts?

_____

(7) Are you attracted to unavailable, mean or indifferent men? Do you date exchange students or foreign men who are here on extended visas?

_____

(8) Do you feel men can't be trusted?

_____

(9) How do men fail to meet your needs?

_____

(10) Do you feel as if men don't want to commit to you?

_____

IDENTIFYING PATTERNS

EXAMINING PAST EXPERIENCES WITH MEN

	#1	#2	#3
1. Were you willing to accept him as he was, or were there any serious flaws? What were they? When were they first noticed?			
2. Was he available for a relationship?			
3. Were you?			
4. Did you marry, live together or date? For how long?			
5. Who pursued?			
6. What attracted you to him in the beginning?			
7. What attracted him to you in the beginning?			
8. Major disagreement?			
9. What was his biggest complaint about you? You of him?			
10. Who ended it?			
11. In what way did he fail to meet your needs? Do you blame him for the relationship failing?			
12. The quality you liked best about him. The worst?			

MY IDEAL MATE

MY IDEAL MATE WOULD HAVE THE FOLLOWING CHARACTERISTICS:

Physical characteristics

1. _____   4. _____

2. _____   5. _____

3. _____   6. _____

Personality traits

1. _____   4. _____

2. _____   5. _____

3. _____   6. _____

Hobbies/talents

1. _____   4. _____

2. _____   5. _____

3. _____   6. _____

My non-negotiable requirements in a mate

1. _____   4. _____

2. _____   5. _____

3. _____   6. _____

PLAN OF ACTION

---

1. How many hours a week am I committed to finding a relationship?

---

2. Have I ended dead-end relationships?

---

3. Do I have a support person in my life?

---

4. What new groups or organizations am I willing to join?

HOW TO ADVERTISE FOR A MATE

Personality descriptions

accomplished
active
adorable
adventurous
affectionate
ambitious
ardent
articulate
artistic
attentive
balanced
bold
bright
brilliant
career-oriented
charming
cheerful
communicative
compassionate
complex
conservative
crazy
creative
cultured
curious
cynical
dependable
doesn't take self too seriously
down to earth
distinguished
dynamic
earthy
East Coast vitality
easy-going
easily amused
effervescent
elegant
energetic
enthusiastic
exciting
expressive

extraordinary
extroverted
exuberant
fantastic
fascinating
feminist
flexible
frank and feisty
fully alive
fun-loving
fun to be with
funny
generous
gentle
gracious
gutsy
happy
have integrity
heartful
high-intensity
high visual appetite
homebody tendencies
honest
impish sense of humor
impulsive
independent
inspiring
intelligent
inventive
irresistible
irreverent
inviting
jovial
laid back
liberal
light-hearted
listener
lively
love to laugh
loyal
magnificent

mature
mellow
mischievous
natural
new age
nonconformist
nonjudgmental
not pushy
old-fashioned
one-of-a-kind
open-minded
opinionated
optimistic
outgoing
original
outrageous
patient
persistent
personable
positive outlook
positive thinker
poised
playful
polite
powerful
quiet
rebel
refined
romantic
saucy
scintillating
secure
self-assured
self-aware
self-entertaining
self-integrated
self-reliant
sense of humor
sensible
sensitive
sensual

HOW TO ADVERTISE FOR A MATE

Personality descriptions (cont.) **Height**   *Eyes*

serious	medium	amber
shy	petite	bedroom eyes
sincere	small	blue-grey
sixties' attitude	statuesque	bright-eyed
socially adept	tall	cobalt
soft	tiny	dark blue
sophisticated	towering	dark eyes
spirited		deep brown
spiritual		green
spontaneous		hazel
stable	*Weight/Shape*	ice blue
stellar		lapis blue
stimulating	athletic	light blue
streetwise	fit	rich brown
strong	full-figured	steel blue
strong-willed	full-hipped	
successful	in good shape	
sultry	in great shape	*Hair*
supportive	large	
sweet	lean	ash blonde
tender	medium build	auburn
thoughtful	muscular	bright red
traditional	nice figure	curly
understanding	on the heavy side	deep red
uninhibited	physically fit	full
unpredictable	plump	honey blonde
unselfish	powerfully built	light brown
urban	proportionate	long
versatile	queen-sized	Orphan Annie
vivacious	Rubenesque	platinum
vulnerable	shapely	salt-and-pepper
warm	slender	sandy blonde
well-rounded	slightly overweight	sandy brown
wise	solid	shiny
witty	trim	short
wonderful	voluptuous	smooth
worldly wise	well-built	steel grey
wry	well-proportioned	straight
young-at-heart	wiry	strawberry blonde
zany		unruly

PERSONALITY PROFILE

Name _____

Age _____

Race _____

Religion _____

Education _____

Marital status _____

Number of dependents _____

EXTERNALS THAT SHAPE YOUR LIVES TOGETHER

Career

- career, success, past, present _____
- career satisfaction? _____
- long term goals, dreams _____
- hours per week? _____
- flexibility? _____
- travel? _____
- high stress?_____

Social history

- social/leisure activities _____
- does he prefer groups or one-on-one? _____
- does he enjoy time alone? _____
- sports _____
- hobbies _____

Family patterns

- birth order _____
- how did the family show appreciation/fight? _____
- duties and responsibilities of mom and dad _____
- relationship with mom and dad _____
- current relationship _____
- socio-economic background _____

PERSONALITY PROFILE

(continued)

Internal functioning

• is he emotionally stable? _____

• what does he like/dislike about himself? _____

• how does he handle anger? _____

    sulker _____

    passive/aggressive _____

    confrontive _____

    violent _____

    holds it in _____

    withholds sex _____

    silent treatment _____

• how does he handle positive feelings? _____

• what upsets him? _____

• what is he looking for in a mate? _____

Individual characteristics (lifestyle/money/habits)

Functioning in a relationship (his track record)

• how long do his relationships last? _____

• how have they ended? _____

• who left? _____

• what are his complaints about the women in his past? _____

_____

• was he faithful? _____

• what has been his "type"? _____

• how is money handled? _____

• are they now friends? _____

Sexual style (frequency/timing/attitudes)

Belief systems that effect compatibility

• political/religious views _____

• ethical/moral stance _____

AVAILABILITY CHART

MARRIED WITH CHILDREN	MARRIED WITHOUT CHILDREN	LONG TERM LIVING ARRANGEMENTS	SEPARATED	DIVORCED	SINGLE
FORGET IT!	• Divorce rate higher among childless couples however, • Childless couples rate higher on overall marital satisfaction than do couples with children	• Absence of marriage could mean reflection of life philosophy • unresolved problems • legal or financial problems	• still legally married • often emotionally unstable • sometimes go back	• How long? • Median remarriage time is 44 months after divorce • Financial issues • Child support? Alimony? • Are you available to co-parent? • If you have children would you want to bring a new family member into their lives? • Bitterness over divorce?	• If dating others you need to assess how entangled he is • Investment of time is a good indication of availability • History of long term relationships is a good sign

---

WATCH OUT FOR . . .

Psychologically unavailable men:

Married to their work

Responsibilities towards elderly parents

Professional bachelor/playboy 45, never married

ROMANCE   MANAGEMENT   WORKSHEET

THE FINAL ANALYSIS

SCREENING OBJECTIVELY FOR YOUR NON-NEGOTIABLE NEEDS

Non-Negotiable Needs:	Candidate A:	Candidate B:
1.		
2.		
3.		
4.		
5.		
6.		
7.		
8.		
9.		
10.		

Compensating factors:	Candidate A:	Candidate B:
1.		
2.		
3.		
4.		